Adolescents,
Family,
and Friends

ADOLESCENTS, FAMILY, AND FRIENDS

Social Support after Parents' Divorce or Remarriage

Kandi M. Stinson

New York
Westport, Connecticut
London

Library of Congress Cataloging-in-Publication Data

Stinson, Kandi M.
    Adolescents, family, and friends : social support after parents'
divorce or remarriage / Kandi M. Stinson.
        p.   cm.
    Includes bibliographical references and index.
    ISBN 0-275-93465-9 (alk. paper)
    1. Children of divorced parents—United States—Social networks.
2. Teenagers—United States—Social networks.   3. Remarriage—United
States.   I. Title.
HQ777.5.S75   1991
306.89—dc20   90-7800

British Library Cataloguing in Publication Data is available.

Library of Congress Catalog Card Number: 90-7800
ISBN: 0-275-93465-9

First published in 1991

Praeger Publishers, One Madison Avenue, New York, NY 10010
An imprint of Greenwood Publishing Group, Inc.

Printed in the United States of America

The paper used in this book complies with the
Permanent Paper Standard issued by the National
Information Standards Organization (Z39.48-1984).

10 9 8 7 6 5 4 3 2 1

Contents

Tables   ix

Preface   xi

1   Introduction   1

   Why Study Adolescent Support Networks?
   Focal Concerns

2   Parental Divorce and Remarriage and
      Adolescent Support Networks   11

   Adolescents and Parental Divorce
   Adolescents and Parental Remarriage
   Measuring Social Support Networks
   Adolescent Social Support Networks

3   The Teenagers and Their Networks   25

   The Families
   The Teenagers and Their Networks
   Variation in Adolescent Support Networks
   Comparison of Adolescent and Parental Networks

4 Adolescents and Their Mothers   37

Mothers as Supports
The Early Effects of Divorce
Life in a Single-Parent Home
Remarriage and the Mother-Adolescent Relationship
Gender, Age, and the Adolescent-Mother Relationship
Conclusions

5 Adolescents and Their Fathers   71

Fathers in Adolescent Support Networks
Fathers and Mothers
Fathers after Divorce
Remarriage, Fathers, and Stepfathers
Conclusions

6 Adolescents and Their Relatives   97

Adolescents and Grandparents
Adolescents and Other Relatives
Divorce, Remarriage, and Kin: Two Hypotheses
Relatives and Divorce
Relatives and Remarriage
Conclusions

7 Adolescents and Their Friends   115

Adolescents' Friendships: Age-Peers
Age, Gender, and Peer Relations
Adolescents' Friendships: Nonrelated Adults
Adolescents and Their Siblings
Parents' Marital Status and Adolescent Friendships
Consequences of Age-Peer and Nonrelated Adult Friendships
Conclusions

8 Implications for Adolescents   135

What Do Adolescent Social Support Networks
    Look Like?

*How Are Adolescent Networks Affected by
Parental Divorce or Remarriage?*

*How Do Network Size and Structure Affect
Adolescent Well-being?*

Implications for Research and Theory

Appendix: Methodology and Interview Schedules   147

Bibliography   161

Index   169

Tables

1 Living Arrangements of Children Under 18 Years Old,
   1970 and 1987   3

2 Selected Demographic Characteristics of
   the Teenagers and Parents   26

3 Kinds and Numbers of People Included in
   the Adolescent Support Networks   30

4 Distribution of Adolescents by Number and
   Kin Position of Living Grandparents   98

Preface

Many people have contributed, directly and indirectly, to the completion of this book. In the early stages of conception Peter Uhlenberg and Sherryl Kleinman at the University of North Carolina offered theoretical insights, methodological advice, and general encouragement. Their unflagging support of my research topic and methodology reinforced my commitment to letting my scholarly work be guided by meaningfulness, not by the ease with which it can be completed. The gentle prodding of Jim McIntosh and Judy Lasker at Lehigh University was highly influential in the completion of an early draft. Without the encouragement and practical advice of Judy Lasker it is unlikely that the manuscript would have been submitted for publication. Thanks go also to Mike Weissbuch and my colleagues at Xavier University for creating an environment in which teaching and scholarly research go hand in hand.

Alison Bricken, Anne Davidson, and colleagues at Praeger have been very helpful in preparing the manuscript. Special thanks go to the 30 adolescents and their parents who consented to be interviewed. They opened their homes to a virtual stranger, made me feel at home, and answered my questions openly and honestly. Certainly this book would not have been possible without their help.

Finally, I have always been somewhat jealous of those spouses and children who appear in prefaces, having made no demands and having apparently offered their unflagging understanding and support for the duration. My family is not exactly like that, but I suspect few are in reality. Spouses and children give support and understanding, but they also demand and need it for themselves. My husband, Rick, and children, Allison and Zachary, have taught me what families are all about. They make it all worthwhile.

Adolescents,
Family,
and Friends

Introduction

In recent years few changes in American families have received as much attention as the increasing divorce rate and the number of children living in single-parent households. The implications of these changes for the well-being of individuals and for the future of families in general have been studied by social scientists and debated by the mass media and the public. A guiding assumption in much of the debate seems to be that divorce disrupts the participants' social relations, leaving them isolated and lacking in necessary physical, emotional, and social support. This may be particularly troublesome in the case of children, whose relationship with at least one parent is likely to be disrupted at a time when the custodial parent's emotional and financial resources are diminished.

The focus of this study is on the social support networks of adolescents as they are affected by the parents' marital status. The central question concerns whether living with both parents, or with a mother only, or with a mother and stepfather is associated with variations in the structure and effectiveness of adolescents' social support networks, and what the implications of these variations are for adolescents' well-being.

The definition of social support network being employed is similar to Garbarino's (1983, p. 5): "a set of interconnected relationships among a group of people that provides enduring patterns of nurturance (in any or all forms) and provides contingent reinforcement for efforts to cope with life on a day-to-day basis." A support network may include formal supports, which have their bases in professional helping services such as therapy groups, and informal supports, which exist outside the established helping services (Richardson and Pfeiffenberger, 1983). Furthermore, informal supports may be organized, with established guidelines and meeting times, such as Parents Without Partners, or unorganized and consisting of more personal interaction, such as that with family, friends, or neighbors (Richardson and Pfeiffenberger, 1983). It is expected that networks vary in the relative numbers of these types of support and in their effectiveness for dealing with various situations.

Few people live their lives in isolation from others. Most individuals are enmeshed in webs of relationships—with family, friends, coworkers, teachers, neighbors, and others. As people move through their lives, they encounter myriad individuals with whom they have limited or extended contact, with whom they build, maintain, and often break relationships. Social scientists for some time have attempted to measure these webs of relations and to determine their impacts on the individuals involved in them. The current interest in network analysis attempts to do this by drawing on a variety of theoretical perspectives and methodologies from anthropology, psychology, and sociology.

People are born into networks of relationships. In most cases an individual's first supportive relationship is with at least one parent. In turn the parent brings the child into interaction with a variety of other support- ive persons, particularly relatives. With increasing age the child's social world expands, especially upon entering school. Here the child forms another set of relations, with teachers and other school personnel, and has the opportunity to build relationships, independently of the parents, with age-peers. Over time the individual continues to take more and more responsibility for constructing and maintaining supportive relationships. As Fischer (1982, p. 4) puts it:

> In general, we each construct our own networks. The initial relations are given us—parents and close kin—and often other relations are imposed upon us—workmates, in-laws, and so on. But over time we become responsible; we decide whose company to pursue, whom to ignore or to leave as casual acquaintances, whom to neglect or break away from. Even relations with kin become a matter of choice; some people are intimate with and some people are estranged from their parents or siblings. By adulthood, people have chosen their networks.

This is not to suggest that people are free to create their networks in any way they desire. Certain constraints are placed on people by virtue of the social contexts in which they move, determining the number and kinds of people with whom they are likely to come into contact. Thus, the composition and functions of the network will change over the life course, as they are affected by life transitions and other environmental contingencies. There is considerable evidence that the composition and structure of a person's network of relations have an impact on behavior and well-being (e.g., see Lee, 1979, or Unger and Powell, 1980, for reviews of the literature), particularly in times of crisis, such as changes in economic circumstances, health problems, or natural disasters (see, e.g., Hill, 1949).

WHY STUDY ADOLESCENT SUPPORT NETWORKS?

Studying adolescent social support networks and their relations to parents' marital status is important from practical, social problems, and theoretical standpoints. From a practical standpoint, it is legitimate to focus on divorce and remarriage from the adolescent's perspective, since increasing numbers of children face the disruption of their parents' marriage every year (Glick, 1979). At any given point in time significant numbers of children are living with a single parent following divorce, as is shown in Table 1. The proportion of children living with a divorced mother increased for both whites and blacks over the 1980s. Indeed, the years between 1970 and 1984 witnessed a doubling of the number of single-parent families in the United States (Norton and Glick, 1986). After examining data from a nationally representative sample of children, Furstenberg and colleagues (1983) found that over a quarter of the children born between 1965 and 1967, and one-third of those born between 1968 and 1969, have

Table 1
Living Arrangements of Children Under 18
Years Old, 1970 and 1987 (percent distribution)

	1970	1987
Percent Living With		
Both Parents	85.2	73.1
Mother Only		
Divorced	3.3	8.5
Married, Spouse Absent	4.7	5.2
Single	0.8	6.3
Widowed	2.0	1.3
Father Only	1.1	2.6
Neither Parent	2.9	2.9

Source: U.S. Bureau of the Census, 1990.

experienced the disruption of their parents' marriage, and estimate that perhaps 60 percent of all children born in 1984 will spend some time in a one-parent family before they turn 18.

Given high rates of remarriage following divorce, it is misleading to think of divorce as a permanent state for most people. About three out of four divorced women and five out of six divorced men remarry (Cherlin, 1981). Additionally, they tend to do it quickly—the median length of time between divorce and remarriage is less than three years (Norton and Moorman, 1987). From the child's perspective, within five years of the parents' divorce, four out of seven white children and one out of eight black children enter a stepfamily (Furstenberg et al., 1983). Cherlin and McCarthy (1985) estimate that one-sixth of all children under 18 years of age in the United States are currently living with a stepparent. Clearly, by the time they are adolescents, many children will experience two or more transitions relating to the divorce and, possibly, remarriage of their parents.

Focusing on variations in support networks related to the mother's marital status is also relevant from a social problems perspective. Since so many children are expected to spend some amount of time in single-parent or remarried households, it is important to have some understanding of the implications of these trends for children's lives. First, divorce and remarriage can be seen as disruptors of social support networks already in existence. Changes and continuities in parent-child relationships, relationships with relatives, and general issues of adjustment and well-being are all relevant concerns in this regard. Second, if social support networks are useful in alleviating some of the stress and disruption that follow divorce, then it is crucial to identify those types of networks which are most effective, and the factors which influence their construction and implementation.

Theoretically, adolescent support networks, as they are affected by parents' marital status, raise several pertinent questions. First, the majority of the support network research has focused on adults rather than on children. Presumably, children are supported directly, instrumentally, and emotionally by their parents and are dependent upon them to bring them into contact with other potentially supportive persons, such as relatives. This implies that, particularly in the case of young children, their support networks should be very similar, if not identical, to those of their parents. However, because of their increased mobility, growing independence, and expanding social worlds, adolescents are in a better position than younger children to initiate their own contacts. At the same time adolescents are not yet adults, and most continue to depend on their parents, at the very least, for physical support. In this sense, adolescents make an interesting case study for exploring the process of social network construction.

A second theoretical interest relates to the usefulness of support networks during times of crisis. Adolescence is a period of physical, psychological, and social transitions. If social support networks are useful during periods of transition, they may be especially critical for adolescents, who are attempting to weather several transitions simultaneously. At the same time, it is expected that the social support networks themselves will be changing during this time as adolescents expand their social worlds and experiment with making and breaking ties, especially in the areas of peer friendships and other-sex relationships. The degree to which adolescents' support networks are unstable, and how this affects their networks' capacity to meet adolescents' needs, are important empirical questions. Thus, focusing on the impacts of adolescent networks during times of transition should complement the research on adult support networks.

A third theoretical issue relates to how one defines network adequacy or usefulness. When focusing on adolescents, defining the adequacy of social support networks becomes particularly problematic. While it is generally agreed that support from friends is important for adults (Fischer, 1982), there is ambivalence with regard to adolescent friendships. On the one hand, it is assumed that having friends and being "popular" are important for self-esteem and well-being (Coleman, 1980). At the same time, there is a fear that age-peers may compete or interfere with other parts of the network, namely, parents (Brittain, 1968, 1969; Larsen, 1972a, 1972b). This fear is seen in the amount of attention paid to the negative aspects of peer pressure among teenagers. Thus, several issues concerning support network adequacy are raised. In terms of adequacy it may be that size is less important than the composition or structure of the network. In the case of adolescents, then, more may be better *only* if it is more of certain kinds of support. Furthermore, when one considers the question of whether a network is adequate, it is probably necessary to ask: Adequate for what? It may be that what makes a network adequate for adolescents may not be suitable for young adults or older individuals. Thus, the definition of adequacy may differ by stage of the life course, since individuals at different points in the life course may have different needs and different personal resources upon which to draw.

Finally, studying adolescent support networks by living arrangements is also theoretically interesting because it draws attention to families as systems of interaction. Divorce and remarriage are transitions that affect families, not just individuals. If adolescents are still in part dependent upon their parents for support directly, as well as indirectly through their connections with other supports, then anything that disrupts or changes the parent-adolescent relationship or the parent's social support network can be expected to affect the adolescent's network. Additionally, changes in adolescents' support networks are expected to affect the parent-adolescent relationship.

FOCAL CONCERNS

Given the exploratory nature and qualitative approach of the study, formal hypotheses are neither formulated nor tested. At the same time, several general questions guide both the research design and the analysis of the data. Furthermore, previous research and theory suggest at least tentative and preliminary answers to these questions.

Size and Structure of Adolescent Support Networks

The first general question of interest is, quite simply: What do adolescent social support networks look like? The size and structure of the network, as well as the kinds of support that are provided, are relevant. Considering their increasing maturity, mobility, and independence, it would seem reasonable to expect adolescents to have networks that are larger than those of younger children. However, their continuing dependence on parents and the restrictions arising from that dependence are likely to have a depressing effect on network size.

The types of people who are likely to be included in adolescent support networks is an open question. Presumably, despite adolescents' greater ability to form social ties independent of their parents, parental support is an important component of adolescent support networks because parents and children share a common residence and their relationship has a rather lengthy history. Given relatively high levels of age segregation, and the emphasis in American society on the nuclear family, it is assumed that adolescents will not have a great deal of contact with nonparental adults, with the possible exception of grandparents. When they do have such contact, it is likely that it will be with adults playing formal roles, such as teachers or counselors or with adults indirectly tied to the adolescents through their parents, such as neighbors or family friends. Finally, it is expected that adolescents will include a relatively high number of age-peers as supports. Particularly, they are expected to serve as emotional supports or confidants, and social companions.

The Effects of Divorce and Remarriage

The second general question of concern is: How are adolescent social support networks affected by the divorce or remarriage of parents? This question focuses our attention on variations in the support networks that can be attributed to variations in living arrangements associated with parents' marital status. Divorce, by definition, involves the disruption of the parents' marriage, which in turn is likely to affect the adolescent's relationship with both parents. Assuming that relationships with parents are central components in the support networks, disruptions in this component can reasonably be expected to have effects throughout the networks.

To the extent that divorce leads to increased stress and decreased resources, including time, energy, and emotional support, the parent-adolescent relationship is expected to be more problematic when the custodial parent is divorced. Furthermore, the amount of interaction between the adolescent and the noncustodial parent will by definition decrease because a residence is no longer being shared. This decrease in interaction is likely to lead to a decreased potential for obtaining emotional support from that parent. It is also expected that since most of the interaction is likely to occur on weekends or during vacation times, interaction with the father is likely to center on entertainment and shared leisure activities, while the custodial mother will bear the brunt of the day-to-day demands of parenting.

The parent-child relationship following divorce is also likely to influence other aspects of the adolescent's support network. Despite high mobility and the voluntary nature of the American kinship system, it is expected that a good deal of interaction between relatives may occur. Relatives, particularly grandparents, may be potential sources of support for adolescents. However, parental divorce may decrease this potential by making it more difficult for adolescents to maintain interaction with the noncustodian's relatives. To some extent, this may depend on the father's willingness to "sponsor" his children with his relatives by taking an active part in initiating and maintaining continued contact between them. At the same time, it is possible that contact will increase with maternal relatives, especially grandparents, particularly if the mother draws on them for increased emotional and instrumental aid. The custodial mother, in fact, may be in a particularly central position to exert a great deal of influence on the adolescent's relationships with kin. Not only is she likely to affect the adolescent's relationship with her own kin, her relationship with her former in-laws is likely to affect the adolescent's relationship with paternal kin.

Overall, divorce may mean not only the loss of some support from the father but also the loss of support from other influential adults, particularly the paternal grandparents. The question that arises then is whether adolescents living with a divorced mother may be especially disadvantaged in terms of adult supports. This leads to the possibility that adolescents living with divorced parents, as well as those who do not have a close relationship with their parents, are especially likely to rely on age-peers to compensate for decreased parental support.

The subsequent remarriage of the mother is likely to affect the mother-adolescent relationship and to have consequences for other parts of the adolescent's support network as well. First, it is possible that remarriage provides a close, emotionally supportive relationship for the mother, and relieves some of the burdens of single parenting, thereby decreasing strain in the mother-adolescent relationship. However, remarriage may actually increase the stress in the mother-child relationship. The presence of a stepfather will require reorganization of the household, which is likely to have an impact on the mother-adolescent relationship. Furthermore, conflict may occur when the mother finds herself in the middle of conflicts and disagreements between the stepfather and the stepchild.

Given the paucity of previous research in this area, it remains an open question as to how the rest of the support network will be affected by the mother's remarriage. It is suspected that the presence of a stepfather will affect the father-adolescent relationship, although it is difficult to predict exactly what those effects will be. On the one hand, the adolescent may draw closer to the biological parent in an effort to withdraw from the stepfather or to express disapproval of the remarriage. On the other hand, it may be more difficult to maintain a close relationship with the noncustodial father when there is an alternative role model and supportive adult in the home. Finally, while remarriage might increase the potential pool of supportive kin by adding a set of "stepkin," it is not expected that stepkin will be important sources of support for a significant number of the teenagers. The assumption is that any interaction which occurs with stepkin will be of a relatively casual nature, particularly if the child is an adolescent at the time of the remarriage.

Adolescent Support Network Adequacy

The final question guiding the research is: What are the impacts of network size and structure on adolescent well-being? Specifically, the focus is on what kinds of networks are most adequate in meeting the needs of the adolescents. It is assumed that network size is relevant, in that the more people one has to draw on, the more reliable the network will be. Thus, if one person is unable or unwilling to provide the needed support, someone else potentially will be available to do so. However, size may not be the only or the most significant aspect of a network's structure in determining the effectiveness of a network for providing needed aid. If the network is relatively homogeneous, there may be a good deal of redundancy in the kinds of support that are provided.

It is further suspected that relationships with some network members will be more important than those with others in determining the adequacy of the networks. For example, the quality of the parent-adolescent relationship, regardless of parents' marital status, may be related to the relative importance of age-peers in adolescents' support networks. Especially following divorce, the parent-adolescent relationship is presumed to have important effects on post-divorce adjustment. The closeness of the divorced mother-adolescent relationship and the amount of contact and the closeness of the relationship with the noncustodial father are expected to affect the adolescent's post-divorce adjustment.

The remainder of this volume will explore the answers to these guiding questions. In order to place the findings in a theoretical and empirical context, Chapter 2 includes a review of the literature concerning adolescent support networks and the impacts of parental divorce and remarriage on adolescent well-being. Chapter 3 provides an overview of the general size and structural characteristics of the networks. The following four chapters each focus on a particular segment of the support networks that emerge as significant sources of support. Chapter 4 focuses on the mother-adolescent relationship, and the father-adolescent relationship is the focal concern of Chapter 5. The adolescents' relationships with relatives, particularly grandparents, is the subject of Chapter 6. In Chapter 7 attention is focused on adolescents' friendships, especially with age-peers but also including those with nonrelated adults. In Chapter 8 we return to the guiding questions and reconsider the tentative answers set forth, in light of the empirical results.

2

Parental Divorce and Remarriage and Adolescent Support Networks

Despite the growing numbers of adolescents who experience the divorce and possible remarriage of their parents, and increasing awareness of the positive impacts of support networks on individuals' well-being, little research has combined consistently an interest in these areas from the adolescent's point of view. This deficit in the previous research makes it difficult to formulate hypotheses. At the same time, it is possible to piece together research that has some bearing on at least one aspect of the problem. Clearly, the research on the effects of parental divorce and adolescents is relevant. It is also helpful to pay some attention to the ways in which adult support networks have been conceptualized and various network characteristics have been measured. While little research has addressed the social support networks of adolescents per se, it is possible to make a few assumptions about what kinds of persons are likely to play significant parts in adolescent support networks.

Thus, research has concentrated on adolescents' relationships with parents and age-peers. Additionally, the continuing dependence of adolescents on their families implies that at least certain kinds of kin may be significant supports. Each of these bodies of literature will be considered for its potential relevance to the relationship between adolescent social support networks and adolescent living arrangements as they relate to parents' marital status.

ADOLESCENTS AND PARENTAL DIVORCE

While the last few decades have witnessed a great deal of research on the effects of divorce and remarriage on children, much of it is methodologically flawed or quite limited in scope. Traditionally research in this area has been based on a deficit model of single-parent families that emphasizes the problems and weaknesses of these families compared with two-parent families. Most commonly the focus is on the negative outcomes associated with the father's absence. The assumption is that fathers directly affect the psychological well-being of their children, especially sons. Therefore, if the father is absent from the home, negative effects will accrue. Father-absence has been expected to have the greatest impacts in the provision of an appropriate sex-role model and paternal supervision and discipline (Longfellow, 1979). The usefulness of the father-absence literature for studying the impact of divorce on children is limited. Assumptions concerning the deviance of father-absent families and their inevitable dysfunctions many times have led to biases and methodological problems, including lumping all single-parent families together, regardless of the cause of father-absence, and the lack of a suitable comparison group of two-parent families (Levitin, 1979). Overall, the findings in this area are inconclusive and contradictory.

Since the early 1970s several major research projects have been designed to overcome the shortcomings of earlier studies, and specifically to study the impact of divorce on children. All four projects have the advantage of being longitudinal in design, and two have the further advantage of utilizing nationally representative samples. While all of these projects have yielded interesting and useful insights into the effects of divorce on children, two of them (Guidubaldi and Cleminshaw, 1985; Guidubaldi et al., 1983; Guidubaldi et al., 1984; Guidubaldi et al., 1986; Guidubaldi, Perry, and Cleminshaw, 1984; Hetherington, Cox, and Cox, 1976, 1978, 1979, 1982) focus on the experiences of younger children, and so will be described only briefly.

The goal of the study undertaken by Hetherington, Cox, and Cox (1976, 1978, 1979, 1982) is to examine families' interaction and reorganization over a two-year period following divorce. Seventy-two white, middle-class preschoolers in the custody of their divorced mothers are matched with 72 children in two-parent homes on the basis of sex, age, and birth order. Multiple methods are used to assess family interaction, including parent interviews, structured diaries by the parents, laboratory observations of parents and children, parent ratings of the children's behavior, observations of the children in nursery school, and various personality scales for the parents.

This study vividly documents the stress experienced by young children in the first year following a divorce (Hetherington, Cox, and Cox, 1976, 1978, 1979). Furthermore, it demonstrates the importance of the child's sex in adjustment to divorce. After two years, adjustment problems have been largely resolved by the girls in their sample, but the boys are still showing signs of psychological maladjustment (Hetherington et al., 1978).

The NASP–Kent State University Impact of Divorce Project began in the early 1980s (Guidubaldi and Cleminshaw, 1985; Guidubaldi et al., 1983; Guidubaldi et al., 1984; Guidubaldi et al., 1986; Guidubaldi, Perry, and Cleminshaw, 1984). Randomly selected school psychologists across the country randomly selected an elementary school in their district, and children from that school in the first, third, and fifth grades, yielding a sample of 699 children, 341 of whom are living with a currently divorced parent and 358 of whom are living with both biological parents. Two years later a follow-up sample consists of 46 children from divorced families and 77 from two-parent families. Multiple methods and instruments are utilized, including psychologists' and teachers' ratings, as well as parents' and children's interviews and standardized instruments.

While outcomes vary by sex and grade level, in general, social and academic adjustments are higher for children living in two-parent households than for children living with a divorced parent (Guidubaldi et al., 1983; Guidubaldi, Perry, and Cleminshaw, 1984). At the same time, the researchers identify several factors that contribute to higher adjustment in children living with divorced parents (Guidubaldi et al., 1986). It appears that positive relationships between the child and both the custodial and the noncustodial parent, particularly with the same-sex parent, as well as a positive relationship between the divorced parents themselves, positively affect child adjustment. Additionally, conflict between the parents and an authoritarian style of child rearing are both negatively related to child adjustment.

The remaining two longitudinal studies are particularly relevant because both include adolescents in their samples. The Wallerstein and Kelly Project (Wallerstein and Kelly, 1974, 1975, 1976, 1977, 1979, 1980; Kelly and Wallerstein, 1975, 1976, 1977) began in 1970 to assess the impact of divorce on each family member shortly after separation, and at follow-ups over a period of several years. The sample consists of 131 children and adolescents between the ages of 2 and 18, from 60 families residing in a suburban northern California county, obtained from referrals by lawyers, schools, community agencies, and self-referred parents. The majority

(92%) are white, with an average family size of 2.2 children. Interviews with the parents and children covered pre-divorce family relationships, parent-child communication during the divorce, and the availability of support systems. Assessments of the child's adjustment are based on reports by the parents, teachers, children, and therapists.

While the study is well designed and carefully executed, caution should be exercised in generalizing the results. The children and parents were seen by an interdisciplinary clinical team at the community health center, in exchange for free counseling. Although the children studied were judged by parents and teachers to be functioning within normal limits, the study is based largely on a clinical design. It is possible that the parents who participate are having problems with their children, a situation making free counseling more attractive. Despite this, the Children of Divorce Project provides many important insights into children's functioning following divorce.

Most important, it is found that children's reactions to divorce vary greatly by age. For preschoolers the typical reactions are fear and confusion, related to an increased sense of vulnerability, sadness over the loss of the absent parent, fear of losing the remaining parent, and guilt (Wallerstein and Kelly, 1975, 1979). The most common feelings of early latency children (ages approximately 7–8) are sadness, loss, and insecurity (Kelly and Wallerstein, 1976). Later latency children (approximate ages 9–10) are distinguished by their intense anger and feelings that their loyalties are divided between their parents (Wallerstein and Kelly, 1976). Adolescents are the most openly upset by the divorce and are most expressive of their feelings of anger, sadness, shame, and embarrassment (Wallerstein and Kelly, 1974). Most of the adolescents experience anger and pain, but they have an advantage over the younger children in that they are better able to understand why the parents separated and are better able to resolve interpersonal conflicts (Wallerstein and Kelly, 1980). Furthermore, adolescents are more likely to seek support from people outside the family, such as peers or school personnel.

In addition to noting the significance of age, Wallerstein and Kelly find that the most distressed children are those whose custodial parents are the most distressed, those who become the focus of their parents' conflicts, and those whose parents receive little emotional support from family and friends. These findings all point to the importance of the parents' adjustment to divorce for the children's adjustment. Wallerstein and Kelly (1979) are quick to point out that there are important differences in the experiences of children and their parents in the aftermath of divorce. While the adults in the sample have settled into a reasonable routine and reached at least a moderate level of adjustment at the end of the first year following the divorce, their children continue to show signs of maladjustment at that time.

The final major longitudinal project of interest is the National Surveys of Children (Furstenberg and Nord, 1985; Furstenberg et al., 1983; Peterson and Zill, 1986). The first wave of the study, conducted in 1976–1977, was comprised of 2,301 children between the ages of 7 and 11 in households chosen in a national probability sampling design. Follow-up data were obtained in 1981 from 1,423 of the children who were between the ages of 12 and 16 at the time. Among the findings of the study to date are that behavior problems among children are more common when the parents' marriage has been disrupted, although this effect is moderated somewhat when the children maintain good relationships with both parents (Peterson and Zill, 1986). Furthermore, behavior problems are most prevalent among children living with the opposite-sex parent (Peterson and Zill, 1986), a finding corroborated by some researchers (Santrock and Warshak, 1979) and not by others (Rosen, 1979).

The data from the National Surveys of Children also indicate that divorce severely affects the relationship between the child and the noncustodial parent following divorce (Furstenberg and Nord, 1985; Furstenberg et al., 1983). Nearly half of the children in the sample have not seen their custodial fathers within the previous year (Furstenberg and Nord, 1985). Furthermore, contact with the noncustodial parent tends to be casual and more socially oriented, whereas the custodial parent, typically the mother, takes on the responsibility of everyday child care. Interestingly, despite the limited contact and casual nature of the relationship, the children generally do not complain about the father-child relationship. While this may be a rationalization to some degree, it is also possible that children, in the words of the authors, apply a "sliding scale" to their relationships, thereby being content with less, given the circumstances (Furstenberg and Nord, 1985).

All of the projects described thus far have the advantage of being longitudinal in design, thereby demonstrating the changes experienced by children and their families over time. Several other studies, conducted either at one point in time or over a much shorter time span, suggest potentially important variables that might mediate the relationship between parental divorce and children's adjustment. Jacobson (1978a, 1978b, 1978c) finds that the amount of time lost with the noncustodial father and hostility between the divorced parents are negatively related to the child's post-divorce adjustment, while parent-child communication concerning the divorce positively affects adjustment. The importance of the parent-child relationship to adjustment is also noted by Hess and Camara (1979), who find that a close relationship between the child and each parent is positively related to post-divorce adjustment, and a close relationship with one parent is better than none. Furthermore, free access to the noncustodial parent positively affects children's adjustment (Rosen, 1979).

While it is fairly clear that good relationships with parents contribute to children's adjustment, it also appears that this may be particularly problematic following divorce. For one thing, cohesion may be lower in one-parent families, especially when the children are younger (Amato, 1987). Additionally, single mothers may experience considerable role strain (Weiss, 1979). Sanik and Mauldin (1986) find that, compared with married mothers, single mothers have the least amount of time for housework, child care, personal care, and volunteer work, especially if they are employed. At the same time, the mothers do not differ in the amount of time spent on nonphysical family care. Whether these conditions lead to more responsibility on the part of the children is not clear. Some researchers indicate that children in one-parent families have high levels of responsibility and autonomy (Amato, 1987; Weiss, 1979). However, Devall and colleagues (1986) find that children in divorced families do not have more responsibilities than other children, nor do they participate in fewer activities, although they perceive themselves as having more responsibilities and fewer involvements than their peers.

Information on the long-term effects of divorce on children and adolescents is particularly limited. There is some evidence that children of divorce and remarriage learn to cope as successfully with life as do their counterparts in intact homes (Kulka and Weingarten, 1979). Others, however, are more cautious in their conclusions. After examining several dimensions of psychological well-being, using the pooled samples from the 1973–1982 General Social Surveys, Glenn and Kramer (1985) find several statistically significant negative effects related to experiencing parents' divorce. This is especially the case for females, some of this effect being due to their greater propensity to divorce.

ADOLESCENTS AND PARENTAL REMARRIAGE

For a large number of children in the United States, living with a divorced parent is a temporary state. Despite some evidence that the likelihood of remarriage following divorce is decreasing (Norton and Moorman, 1987), approximately one-sixth of all children in two-parent households are living with a stepparent (Norton and Glick, 1986). At the same time, negative stereotypes of remarriage and stepparents abound, affecting both the popular literature on stepfamilies and the scholarly literature. An examination of 11 self-help books for children or adolescents finds that the books cite more problems with stepfamilies than strengths, including what to call the stepparent, differences in family styles, loyalty conflicts, and discipline (Coleman and Ganong, 1987). Focusing on problems encountered also appears to characterize popular magazine articles between 1940 and 1980 (Pasley and Ihinger-Tallman, 1985), in part because they draw on the clinical literature to a greater extent than on the empirical literature. These stereotypes are also likely to affect stepfamily members themselves. Fine (1986) indicates that college students perceive stepparents less positively than natural parents, and only in the case of perceptions of stepmothers does living with a stepparent have any effect on stereotypes.

Generalizability of research findings on stepfamilies is severely limited because of the predominance of clinical designs and data bases in the literature. Thus, Ganong and Coleman (1986) suggest that empirical studies tend to find few differences between stepchildren and children in other types of families, whereas clinical studies focus on stepfamilies' problems and difficulties, and the subsequent maladjustment of the children. For example, Visher and Visher (1979) suggest that much of the stress encountered in stepfamilies is due to the continuance of pre-remarriage bonds, such as with the ex-spouse and biological parent; incomplete mourning for the ex-spouse or biological parent; and the continuing presence and influence of the noncustodial parent. However, the empirical research has suggested that frequent contact with the ex-spouse and biological parent does not negatively affect the quality of the remarriage relationship (Clingempeel and Brand, 1985), nor does it negatively affect the stepfather-stepchild relationship (Pink and Wampler, 1985).

The tendency to emphasize negative findings is prevalent. For example, on the basis of a large-scale survey, Bowerman and Irish (1962) find a number of differences between stepchildren and those in nuclear families, including lower affection and closeness expressed for stepparents than for biological parents, and more frequent feelings of parental rejection on the part of stepchildren. Despite the fact that the findings of this particular study are contradicted by the majority of stepparent-stepchild research studies, it is often cited as a "classic" study and is one of the most frequently cited in family textbooks (Nolan et al., 1984).

When the stepfamily research is considered as a whole, despite the finding that remarried individuals are more likely to feel inadequate in their family role performance (Weingarten, 1980), there is little evidence that children in stepfamilies differ from other children on a wide range of variables, including school performance, intelligence, psychosomatic symptoms, personality characteristics, family relationships, and attitudes about marriage (Ganong and Coleman, 1984). Indeed, at least one study finds that the presence of a stepfather may mitigate the possible harmful effects of father-absence (Oshman and Manosevitz, 1976). Also, after administering questionnaires to adolescents from both step and nuclear families, Bohannon (1979) finds that stepchildren perceive themselves to be just as happy and well adjusted as their nuclear family counterparts.

It is possible that the stepfamily research suffers from biases and untested assumptions similar to those characterizing the research on the effects of divorce. In the case of stepfamilies, however, the problem arises not from a part that is lacking but from a part that does not fit. What is needed is a new model that sees the stepfamily as a viable arrangement and focuses on the factors which affect stepfamily functioning, and the ways in which stepfamilies adapt and cope.

At the very least it appears that adjustment to a stepparent may be affected by the age and sex of the stepchild. Stepfathers are more likely to form positive relationships with stepchildren when the children are young and eager to have a stepfather (Visher and Visher, 1978). Several researchers (Hetherington et al., 1982; Wallerstein and Kelly, 1980) find that young boys in particular may attach rapidly to stepfathers and form intense and warm relationships with them. On the other hand, girls display less warmth toward their stepfathers (Santrock et al., 1982), and in a laboratory problem-solving task demonstrate more negative behavior toward their stepfathers even though stepparents do not distinguish between the boys and the girls in their responses (Clingempeel et al., 1984).

The stepparent-stepchild relationship may also depend to some extent on the quality of the remarriage relationship. Brand and Clingempeel (1987) find that for stepfathers, a more positive marital relationship is associated with more positive perceptions of the stepchildren; the same effect is not found for stepmothers. Additionally, stepfamily adjustment and functioning may vary by structural characteristics of the family. Stepparenting may be more positive when the stepparent and stepchild share a residence, as opposed to visiting occasionally (Ambert, 1986). Furthermore, marital quality appears to be lower in complex remarriages, in which both spouses have been previously married, than in situations where only one has been married before (Clingempeel and Brand, 1985). Finally, couples in complex remarriages are less likely than other remarried couples to be integrated into an extended kin network, although other aspects of community integration do not vary by remarriage structure (Ihinger-Tallman and Pasley, 1986).

MEASURING SOCIAL SUPPORT NETWORKS

Social networks have been conceptualized in a variety of ways, depending in part on one's theoretical perspective and the aspects of social networks in which one is interested. Traditionally, anthropologists have focused on "personal networks," with ego at center, surrounded by a variety of persons with whom ego has emotional, instrumental, or informational ties. Usually the focus is on the impact of various network configurations on ego's behavior. A classic example of this approach is Bott's (1971) study of the relationship between network density and conjugal roles. Psychologists, particularly sociometrists, have derived their own version of network analysis from graph theory, the mathematical analysis of the relationships between points on a graph. Studies of children's friendship choices and cliques are illustrations of this approach. Sociologists, in their studies of networks, tend to concentrate on structural systems and the relationships between positions. Thus, hierarchies of control, informational flows, and the distribution of resources tend to be primary concerns.

The particular approach chosen influences how social networks are measured as well as how they can be described and analyzed. When the focus is on personal networks, a common technique for gathering data is "name elicitation," in which respondents are asked a broad question about the persons from whom they obtain support (Fischer, 1982). In his classic statement on conceptualizing relevant network characteristics, Mitchell (1969) distinguishes two categories of network characteristics: morphological aspects refer to the relationship or patterning of the links in the network with respect to one another, while interactional aspects refer to the nature of the links themselves.

Three morphological criteria are of particular relevance. The point of anchorage of a network is the starting point from which the network is traced, that is, the individual whose behavior is being interpreted. The second important criterion is range or size, which is the number of persons in direct contact with the person on whom the network is anchored. A third morphological characteristic of interest is density, the extent to which possible links actually exist, often measured as the ratio of actually observed ties to potential ties.

Network density is associated with the amount of social control that can be brought to bear upon ego. Dense or closely knit networks, in which members are likely to know and have ties with each other, appear better able than less dense or loosely knit networks to mobilize and bring their resources to bear upon ego's behavior or attitudes. Bott (1971) finds that married couples with dense networks are more likely to have a high degree of sex segregation in their activities and household division of labor. It has been found that after divorce, women who want to maintain a traditional role are best served by a dense network, whereas women who want to change their traditional role orientations are best served by a loosely knit network (McLanahan et al., 1981).

Three of the interactional criteria identified by Mitchell (1969) are important. The first is content, which can be divided into various aspects, one of which relates to the meanings that persons in the network attribute to their relationship or the kind of support that is provided. The content of supportive ties itself can be categorized into several broad groups: emotional, consisting of psychological types of support, such as serving as a confidant, listening to one's problems, or just "being a friend"; instrumental, including a range of concrete services, such as lending money, baby- or house-sitting, or helping with household chores; and informational, consisting of acting as a source of useful information or advice, or providing helpful contacts (Unger and Powell, 1980). Other researchers include companionship as another type of support, largely in the form of acting as someone with whom social activities or interests can be shared (Fischer, 1982). The other aspect of content is the degree of multiplexity, that is, the extent to which the relationship has more than one content. The second interactional criterion is directedness, which concerns whether the support flows in just one direction or is reciprocated. Finally, frequency refers to the regularity of contact between members of the network.

ADOLESCENT SOCIAL SUPPORT NETWORKS

There is evidence that social support networks may help adults adjust to divorce and deal with single parenting, and may have at least an indirect impact on their children. At the time of a divorce, one's network is in a state of transition as individuals drop out and perhaps others are added. Leslie and Grady (1985) find that in the first year following divorce, women's networks increase in density and in the extent of family membership. It appears that friendship and in-law ties are most subject to change, whereas those based on obligation and family loyalty are more stable (Bowen and Orthner, 1986; McLanahan et al., 1981).

Mental and physical health appear to be higher among single-parent families with larger social support networks (Hanson, 1986; Loveland-Cherry, 1986). Also, the support that divorcing persons receive from kin decreases mood disturbances and has a positive effect on life satisfaction (Berman and Turk, 1981). This may indirectly affect the parent-child relationship. Hetherington, Cox, and Cox (1978) find that contact with relatives and close friends enhances a mother's effectiveness in dealing with her children. It seems that having effective supports upon which one can draw removes some of the responsibility and stress experienced by the single mother, thereby leading her to be more relaxed and effective in interactions with her children (Christensen and McDonald, 1976).

Caution is necessary in interpreting these findings. Some researchers find that network size significantly predicts divorce adjustment for men but not for women (Plummer and Koch-Hattem, 1986). In addition, certain kinds of support may be more useful for coping with some problems than with others. Among low-income single parents, support from friends, neighbors, and community has a significant effect on all dimensions of well-being, whereas support from relatives is useful in dealing with total problems and alleviating isolation, but has no effect on reducing loneliness or increasing happiness (Gladow and Ray, 1986). Colletta (1979) suggests that satisfaction with support, and not support per se, leads to less authoritarian and more responsive behavior on the part of divorced mothers. Thus, it may be that the particular size or structure of a network is less important than its ability to meet the needs and expectations of the focal person.

Virtually no research has examined adolescent social support networks as a whole and considered their impact on adolescent behavior and well-being. Limited research suggests that support networks may help children cope with parental divorce. Concerning children's use of resources for support, it has been suggested that friends, siblings, classmates, teachers, grandparents, cousins, neighbors, and parents of good friends are all possible sources of support for children after divorce (Kurdek, 1981). Wallerstein and Kelly (1980) find that help-seeking by children after divorce may be a generalized reaction, in that children who turn to parents for help are also likely to turn to friends and teachers. However, they also find that the availability of support systems outside the immediate family has only a very limited effect on post-divorce adjustment for children. Much of the research, however, is only indirectly relevant and examines only specific components of the network, such as relations with parents or conflicts between parents and peers. Nonetheless, some attempt will be made to describe those aspects of adolescent social support networks which are assumed to be most significant.

For a majority of adolescents their relationship with parents is a central part of their social support network. Continuing physical dependence, a shared residence, and emotional bonds that develop throughout childhood will result in some degree of closeness. However, during the teenage years children begin grappling with forming an identity and existence independent of their parents. The inevitable biological differences between middle-aged parents and their adolescent children, as well as the lack of clear, societal norms for relinquishing power and authority, have led many to assume that a "generation gap" is inevitable (Davis, 1940), if not in reality, at least in perceptions (Bengtson and Kuypers, 1971). Some have gone so far as to suggest that youths and their parents operate within entirely different subcultures (Coleman, 1961).

Despite the apparent logic of the argument, there is very little evidence to support the notion of an inevitable generation gap. A review of the literature concludes that there is a great deal of value similarity between parents and youths, and where differences do occur, generally in the areas of sexuality and gender roles, they are differences in degree and not of direction (Troll and Bengtson, 1979). Overall, most parent-adolescent relationships are warm and close, and when conflict does occur, it is usually mild and centers on such issues as curfews or clothing styles (Douvan and Adelson, 1966).

Besides being viable sources of support themselves, parents can serve as links to other supports, namely, relatives. In her study of a lower-class black community, Stack (1974) suggests that fathers act as "sponsors" for their children in relationships with their kin. Men who acknowledge children as their own provide those children with a set of kin that contributes to their support. Paternal kin are less likely to take an interest in and provide support for a child when the man denies paternity. Similarly, after divorce, contact with the custodial parent's kin either stays the same or increases, while contact with the noncustodian's kin tends to decline (Anspach, 1976; Spicer and Hampe, 1975). Furthermore, it is easier for grandparents to continue interacting with grandchildren after divorce if their child, rather than their child-in-law, has custody (Matthews and Sprey, 1984).

Very little research examines adolescent-kin relationships in general. Much of the work on grandparenting examines it from the perspective of the older generation, and is largely an attempt to delineate the components of the grandparent role or to develop a typology of grandparenting styles (Kivnick, 1982; Robertson, 1977). Less is known about the importance to grandchildren of having grandparents, although it appears that the relationship with grandparents can be a close and meaningful one (Barranti, 1985; Kornhaber and Woodward, 1981; Updegraf, 1968). Matthews and

Sprey (1985) distributed questionnaires to 132 late adolescents concerning their relationships with their grandparents. Overall, adolescents are close to their grandparents, although usually to specific ones. Kinship position turns out to be more important than the sex of the grandparent, with grandchildren reporting closer relationships with their maternal grandparents than with their paternal grandparents. In general, grandparents may aid their adolescent grandchildren in developing an identity, dealing with their parents, and developing positive attitudes toward aging (Baranowski, 1982). The roles that are played by other relatives in providing support to adolescents are yet to be seen.

The component of adolescent social support networks that probably receives the most attention is peer relations. Of some concern is the possibility that peers and parents compete for the adolescent's loyalty. The empirical research, however, does not bear this out. First of all, teens tend to choose friends from backgrounds quite similar to their own and, second, peers and parents may complement each other in the sense that they are drawn upon as models or supports in different areas (Brittain, 1968, 1969; Larsen, 1972a, 1972b; Sebald, 1986).

Peer relationships may fulfill several functions during adolescence. Friendships with peers can promote one's self-esteem and confidence, provide models for dating, and supply people with whom to enjoy activities (Coleman, 1980; Douvan and Adelson, 1966). However, the structure and function of adolescent friendships appear to be affected by both the sex and the age of the adolescent. While early adolescents (ages 11–13) stress common activities with friends, middle adolescents (ages 14–16) tend to focus on security, loyalty, or giving help (Douvan and Adelson, 1966; Bigelow and LaGaipa, 1975). It is not until late adolescence (ages 17 and above) that emphasis is placed on the individuality of the friend as well as on the mutuality of the relationship (Douvan and Adelson, 1966). Boys tend to focus more on gang activities and less on personal qualities like sensitivity or empathy than do girls (Douvan and Adelson, 1966). Also, girls appear to be less open to newcomers to a group and more prone to jealousies and tensions in their friendships (Coleman, 1974; Feshbach and Sones, 1971).

Some teenagers may receive support from more organized or formal sources. There is growing interest among counselors and other practitioners in using support networks as a means of dealing with adolescent problems. Some schools are attempting to use peer support groups and other types of school-based networks to deal with problems such as drug abuse and alcoholism (Asp and Garbarino, 1983). Using social support networks to prevent and decrease juvenile delinquency has also received attention (Hawkins and Fraser, 1983). Much is still unknown about the incidence of these networks, how adolescents are recruited into them, and their impacts on behavior and well-being.

What we learn from previous research, limited as it may be, is that social support networks may be important resources for adolescents, particularly those who are coping with the divorce or remarriage of their parents. Parents, grandparents, age-peers, and others are likely to forge close ties with the adolescent, who can draw on those relationships for physical and nonphysical support. At the same time, divorce and remarriage are transitions likely to have significant impacts on the entire family, including their social support networks. Some ties are likely to be broken, others will be added, and many will undergo qualitative changes as members deal with new needs, under a changed set of circumstances. Thus, it is expected that adolescents' social support networks will vary by their living arrangements, as defined by parents' marital status. To what extent this is true, and whether it makes any difference for adolescents, is yet to be seen.

3

The Teenagers and Their Networks

Between December 1982 and January 1984, in-depth, open-ended interviews were conducted with 30 teenagers between the ages of 13 and 17, and their custodial parents. The adolescents were contacted through word-of-mouth referrals and a snowball sampling design, described in detail in the appendix. The families are evenly distributed among three household types: those headed by parents in their first marriage (referred to hereafter as married households), those headed by a divorced mother who has not remarried (divorced households), and those headed by a divorced mother who has remarried and a stepfather (remarried households).

Given the nonrandom way in which participants were chosen, the families are not representative of American families in general. At the same time, the strengths and problems discovered in the families, the issues they face, and the strategies they creatively construct for coping provide some idea of the variety of interaction patterns characterizing families today. All 16 female and 14 male teenagers in the sample are white. At the time of the interviews, all of the families were residing in a midsize Southern town and its vicinity. Major employers in the town include a large state university and a hospital. Outlying areas contain several major research facilities as well as high-technology industries. In close proximity are a midsize city and the state capital.

THE FAMILIES

Selected demographic characteristics of the teenagers and their parents are summarized in Table 2. On the average there are few differences among the three household types, with the exception of median family income. The average ages of the three groups of teenagers are quite similar, as is the average family size. Adolescents living in remarried households have only slightly more siblings than the others, despite the inclusion in the figures of half siblings and stepsiblings residing in the household. It is possible that divorce depresses the fertility rates of those mothers who have not remarried (Norton and Moorman, 1987). However, the average number of children in the married households does not differ much from the others. It is likely that the relatively low number of children in the families has more to do with social class than with the parents' marital status. Twenty-seven of the teens attend public junior high schools or high schools in the area, with the remaining three attending a small, private, church-affiliated school.

The families range from lower-middle- to upper-middle-class, charac-

Table 2
Selected Demographic Characteristics of the Teenagers and Parents

| | | HOUSEHOLD TYPE | | |
	Total	Married	Divorced	Remarried
Teenagers				
Mean Age	15.2	15.1	14.8	15.0
Mean Number of Siblings	1.4	1.4	1.2	1.7
Average Years of Education				
Father	15.6	16.2	15.0	15.5
Mother	13.9	12.9	14.1	14.8
Stepfather	15.7	—	—	15.7
Median Family Income				
in Thousands	30.2	34.7	19.4	36.4
Mean Length in Years				
Current Marriage	12.5	18.2	—	3.0
Since Divorce	8.0	—	6.5	10.5

Note: Average years of education completed by noncustodial fathers is based on mothers' reports and may not be as accurate as the self-reports of mothers and stepfathers.

terized by relatively high levels of parental education and high family incomes. On the average, mothers have completed fewer years of schooling than their spouses, either former or current. While this pattern is not unusual, the largest difference in education is seen among spouses in married households. One possible explanation for this is detected in the following account:

> I was so traditional, I guess now it sounds almost stereotypical. I met my ex-husband when I was a freshman in college. We got married that summer and I dropped out. The next summer my oldest daughter was born. I was a full-time mom and housekeeper and at the time it seemed pretty normal. Even if I had wanted to do something else, it would've been hard. Ted [ex-husband] was career military, and we were very lucky if we were in the same place for two years in a row. Oh, boy, did reality ever hit when we split. I had no degree and absolutely no work experience—I hadn't even had a part-time job in high school. So one of the first things I did, really for survival, was start taking classes at a local college, with a great deal of help from my mom and dad. It took almost seven years going part-time, but I got my degree. (mother of 15-year-old daughter)

A similar story is told by a remarried mother of a 14-year-old daughter:

> When my husband left, it's not like I had a choice. I had to get a job, and the only thing I could find was as a nurse's aide in a nursing home. The work was lousy and the money was worse. There's no way I was going to do that forever, so I started working on a nursing degree.

In one form or another the story is repeated often. Pushed by circumstances into the labor force, many of the divorced mothers enter for the first time, or return to, college in order to increase their earning power.

Despite their higher levels of education, the divorced mothers have total family incomes substantially lower than those of the married and remarried mothers. This is due in part to the reliance of divorced women on one income, whereas in the majority of the other cases the total family income is based on the earnings of both the husband and the wife. In all three household types the majority of the mothers are employed at least part-time. However, the employment circumstances of the divorced women differ from those of the other women. While the divorced mothers are less likely to be working part-time than the other mothers, when they do, their earnings are the family's major source of income. Furthermore, two of the divorced mothers are full-time graduate students. In some cases the incomes are supplemented by child support from the ex-spouse or gifts and loans from family, but this never exceeds their earnings. Half of the divorced mothers report having received welfare for at least some period of time since their divorce.

Another factor in the income discrepancies among the three household types has to do with the respondents' occupations, which, in the case of divorced women, tend to be their major, if not sole, source of income. Both men and women in the sample do have relatively good jobs, primarily white-collar, compared to traditionally blue-collar jobs such as factory work and unskilled labor. At the same time, the white-collar jobs held by the women have relatively lower levels of education and income compared to the white-collar jobs held by the men. For example, nursing and medicine are both considered white-collar, professional occupations. However, doctors have more education and earn considerably more than nurses. Furthermore, the vast majority of nurses are female while the majority of doctors are male.

Obviously the sample is biased in terms of racial and social class composition, and probably in other ways as well. The ten divorced mothers who have not remarried have been divorced an average of a little over six years. Given that the majority of divorced women remarry, and about half of them do so within three years of the divorce (Cherlin, 1981), it is possible that these women who have not remarried are not representative of divorced women in general. Indeed, this is somewhat corroborated by the reports of the divorced mothers themselves. Only two of the currently divorced women would like to remarry. Two others are considering cohabiting without marriage. Differences are seen when the divorced mothers reflect on their current states. Despite monetary hardships and the overload and stress associated with single parenting, the mothers generally describe themselves as emotionally better off compared with their married years. This contrasts with the currently remarried women, who say they are currently better off than they were when they were divorced, citing fewer money problems, help with child rearing, and the companionship afforded by a spouse.

It is possible that these differences are simply rationalizations of their current statuses. However, differences also emerge when the divorced and remarried mothers are compared on their accounts of the problem issues in their first marriages. Since the interviews do not focus on the circumstances surrounding the first marriages, information is not available for all of the women. Thus, caution in interpreting these patterns is advised. Nonetheless, some typical responses do occur:

I think the rules [of marriage] are stacked against us [women]. Maybe this is an exaggeration, but I know I felt like I was the one that was doing all the giving, and he was getting. From looking at the women I know, it doesn't seem that different for them. (divorced mother of 16-year-old son)

Marriage is such a heavy thing. As long as you're not married, you're still two people. There's something that's just yours. But as soon as you make it official, bang, you're gone. You're a couple, and that's it. (divorced mother of 14-year-old daughter)

My ex-husband was not a great communicator. He's still not. A lot of our problems just got worse and worse because they were bottled up. Don's [current husband] so different. We really talk. (remarried mother of 16-year-old daughter)

When we got married, we were incredibly immature. Just out of high school, I was pregnant, no money. It was doomed. (divorced mother of 14-year-old son)

In general, remarried mothers' complaints center on specific characteristics of themselves, their spouses, or their relationships. In fact, an active effort is made to distinguish the current spouse and marriage from the first. On the other hand, divorced mothers focus on problems with the institution of marriage rather than with their specific marriages. Unfortunately, the cross-sectional nature of this study precludes determining the processes whereby these differences emerge.

It is worth pointing out that the intent of this particular study is not to draw generalizations about a larger population. Rather, the intent is to gather as much in-depth information as possible, and to explore the patterns that occur in this specific group of families. It is assumed that the reported findings can stimulate hypotheses concerning the relationship between household type and adolescents' support networks that could be quantitatively tested with a more representative sample.

THE TEENAGERS AND THEIR NETWORKS

The individual adolescents interviewed are the major points of anchorage of their support networks. Thus, each adolescent is taken as ego and then his or her supportive relationships are traced from that starting point. Only direct ties are considered, that is, only those people who can be approached directly rather than through an intermediary. Also, the parents and stepparents interviewed are considered the points of anchorage of their

Table 3
**Kinds and Numbers of People Included in
the Adolescent Support Networks**

	Number of Teenagers Naming at Least One	Average Number Named
Kind of Person		
Nuclear Family		
Mother	27	1.0
Father	17	1.0
Stepparent	5	1.0
Sibling	6	1.0
Extended Kin		
Grandparents	18	1.5
Aunts or Uncles	5	1.0
Other	3	1.0
Age-Peers	30	3.1
Nonrelated Adults		
Teachers	7	1.4
Other School Personnel	10	1.0
Other Nonrelated Adults	9	1.0

respective networks so that some comparisons can be made between the parental and adolescent networks.

The range or size of the networks is considered in two ways. First, the overall average number of people who are included in the support networks is calculated. Second, the different kinds or categories of people mentioned can be ascertained and the average number of people in each category calculated. This information is summarized in Table 3. The average range of the networks is between 8 and 9, which is relatively low compared with adult social networks. In his Northern California Community Study, Fischer (1982) found the average size of adult networks to be slightly over 18 people. In this study the average size of the mothers' networks is approximately 15 people, while fathers average a little over 12 persons. At the same time, there is considerable variation in the sizes of the adolescent support networks, ranging from a low of 2 to a high of 23 people.

There is also variation in the kinds of people named. The most commonly named supports, in terms of both likelihood of inclusion and average number named, are age-peers, followed by parents, particularly mothers. Grandparents are also frequently mentioned sources of support, being named by over half of the respondents. Age-peers are the only category of supportive individuals in which the adolescents are likely to name more than one in the support network. Nonrelated adults are not named frequently, but when they are, they are likely to be school personnel, usually teachers. Overall, if network members are divided into adults and age-peers, there seems to be a preponderance of adults. This is somewhat misleading, however, since all of the adolescents are currently living at home, and thus still dependent upon at least one parent. When parents are left out of consideration, the difference between adults and age-peers is quite small.

It is possible that network density has implications for adolescent behavior, perhaps in the areas of conformity, initiation into deviant activities, or value similarity with parents. In this study density is not directly measured, although it can be roughly inferred from other information. If density is taken to mean the proportion of network members who know and/or have ties with each other, then there is a relatively high degree of density in the adolescent networks, at least in some segments. The most commonly mentioned adults in the support networks are parents and other relatives, especially grandparents. Presumably in this segment of the network density is high because it is reasonable to expect that these individuals will know and have supportive relationships with each other. Indeed, it is this part of the network that is generally "given" to adolescents by their parents. Furthermore, among those adolescents who name more than one age-peer (over two-thirds), it is very common to describe them as a group with a large number of joint activities and interests. Even when friends are singled out as "best friends," they are likely to know the adolescent's other friends and to interact with them fairly frequently. The denseness of the adolescent networks is not surprising, considering that the teens are still fairly limited in their ability to initiate ties independently of their parents. Family and school remain the two most important contexts of adolescent social life. When teenagers do have supportive relationships outside their circle of relatives, they are likely to be with persons met and interacted with in the context of school.

As far as the content of supportive ties goes, the adolescents receive a wide variety of support from the individuals in their networks. The adolescents describe examples of emotional, instrumental, and informational support, although emphasis is placed on emotional support, possibly due to the line of questioning used in the interviews. Typical kinds of emotional support include having someone to talk to and share activities with, and in whom to confide. Instrumental support includes giving or loaning money, providing material needs such as clothing or school supplies, and being a source of transportation. Informational support is the least commonly received from network members, but occasionally adolescents mention asking network members for information related to a problem or decision, such as future college attendance.

An additional aspect of content, multiplexity, refers to whether the ties between network members contain one or more than one kind of support. Overall there is a good deal of division of labor between network members, so that most of the ties are uniplex. The exception is ties with mothers, which, in the majority of cases, include a variety of instrumental aids— such as cooking, cleaning, chauffeuring, or providing money—as well as emotional support in the form of dealing with everyday problems or acting as a confidante, in addition to occasionally providing informational support. Relationships with fathers also tend to be multiplex, although it is difficult to classify fathers' support into the categories described above. Fathers often serve as authority figures or achievement motivators, and only rarely as confidants or persons with whom to talk about problems. Since most of the adolescents' instrumental needs are being met by their parents, most of their other relationships are characterized by emotional support of one sort or another. There is a further division in the sense that even though emotional support is obtained from a variety of people, the adolescents distinguish between people on the basis of the kinds of things they talk about and how personal they feel they can be. Finally, ties with nonrelated adults often start with those adults as sources of informational or instrumental support, due to a common interest or activity, but then evolve into a relationship that includes emotional support.

Directedness is the degree to which support flows in one direction versus two. While one might expect mutual ties to be stronger because each party has obligations and responsibilities to the other, this is not exactly the case in parent-adolescent relationships. With the exception of divorced mothers, support almost always flows from the parent to the adolescent. Obviously other kinds of ties are important in binding parents to their children besides mutual obligations and rights. Although directedness is not measured directly, it appears that in the majority of nonparental relationships the ties are mutual. Thus, most of the adolescents feel that the people they consider friends also rely on them as a person with whom to talk and share activities and interests.

Finally, the overall frequency of contact with network members is high. Once again this relates to the fact that most of a teenager's time is spent in the contexts of home and school. Thus, contact with custodial parents occurs on a daily basis and contact with age-peers almost as frequently.

Divorce considerably decreases the frequency of contact with the noncustodial parent. On the average, teenagers see their noncustodial fathers about once every one or two weeks, although there is a good deal of variation, including no contact and having minimal face-to-face contact for nine months but then living together for the entire summer. Contact with relatives and nonrelated adults varies in frequency, although it is generally less frequent than with parents and age-peers.

In sum, adolescents describe generally small networks that tend to draw on the contexts of family and school for members. The most common type of support received is emotional, particularly in the form of having someone to talk with and confide in concerning problems. Overall, the teens' networks appear to be relatively dense, with the majority of the ties being uniplex and mutual.

VARIATION IN ADOLESCENT SUPPORT NETWORKS

The adolescents' support networks vary both morphologically and interactionally. Some of this variation is clearly and systematically related to the sex and age of the adolescent, and the parents' marital status. It is these variations, particularly those related to parents' marital status, that are the focus of the following four chapters. Thus, they will not be dealt with thoroughly and in detail here; rather, just a few of the highlights will be noted.

There are few gender differences in any of the network characteristics considered, and when they do occur, they often interact with age or parents' marital status. Size and density do not vary by gender. Girls are more likely than boys to confide in their mothers, but only in the married households. Concerning peer relations, boys are more likely to run in groups and draw few distinctions between friends, whereas girls are more likely to have one particularly close "best friend." There is also a gender effect in the sense that both boys and girls demonstrate a strong preference for same-sex choices in the areas of relationships with age-peers, siblings, and nonrelated adults.

Older adolescents have slightly smaller networks than younger adolescents, largely due to the tendency for older teens to have one or two particularly close friends, whereas younger teens tend to be part of a larger, more loosely knit friendship group. Although older teens have fewer friends, they have closer, more intimate relationships with them. The mother-adolescent relationship also varies by adolescent's age, with older adolescents, and possibly firstborns in particular, having a closer relationship with the mother and being more likely to confide in her. However, this is the case only in the married families. When the mother is divorced or remarried, neither the age nor the sex of the adolescent seems to have an impact on the mother-adolescent relationship.

The largest differences in network structure and relationships are associated with the parents' marital status. Teens in divorced and remarried households have slightly larger networks than teens in married households. This is somewhat surprising, since contact with fathers, as well as with other paternal relatives, decreases after the parents' divorce. Two explanations seem reasonable. First, frequency of contact is only one aspect of network structure. Paternal grandparents are only slightly less likely to be seen as supports than are maternal grandparents, even though all of the teens in divorced households are living with their mothers. It seems that the grandparent-grandchild relationship is a particularly close one and can remain so even under conditions of more difficult and less frequent interaction. The second explanation is that teens in divorced and remarried households are more likely to include nonrelated adults in their support networks in addition to, rather than instead of, age-peers, parents, and relatives. While one might expect teens in remarried households to have even larger networks due to the possibility of including stepkin, only a few teenagers rely on stepkin for support.

Parents' marital status also affects adolescent relationships with the mother and father. Divorce affects both the frequency of contact and the content of the ties with fathers. Compared with custodial fathers, noncustodial fathers see their children less and, overall, have less interaction of any type with them. Furthermore, the type of support provided by divorced fathers tends to be of the social, companionship variety, focused on joint, pleasurable activities and outings, and on gift-giving. As far as mothers are concerned, the most significant impact on the networks is in the mutuality of the ties. Divorced mothers particularly, followed by remarried mothers, are more likely not only to provide support for their adolescent children but also to receive emotional support from them. This extends to viewing their children as confidants, a situation that never arises when the biological parents are currently married.

In sum, the morphological aspects of the teenagers' networks are affected minimally by the factors of adolescent's age and sex, and mother's marital status. Teens living with a divorced mother have slightly larger and slightly less dense networks than other teens, due primarily to the inclusion of nonrelated adults. However, overall the differences are not large. Most of the variations identified are in the interactional aspects of the networks, with content and mutuality of the ties most likely to be affected. The exact effect, however, depends to a large extent on which relationship is being considered.

COMPARISON OF ADOLESCENT
AND PARENTAL NETWORKS

Several questions pertaining to similarities and differences between adolescent and parental networks are of theoretical interest. If support networks are viewed as a developmental phenomenon that changes both interactionally and morphologically over time, adolescent networks are a valuable case study for identifying and understanding how people go about constructing personal networks. Furthermore, many questions pertaining to parent-adolescent relationships, such as the degree of value similarity between parents and their children, or the extent to which parents and peers compete for an adolescent's loyalty, lead to a consideration of how much overlap there is between the parents' and the adolescent's networks in terms of membership.

When adolescent networks are compared with adult networks, several things stand out. On average, mothers have networks that are almost twice as large as those of the teenagers. Fathers have networks somewhat smaller than those of the mothers but larger than those of the teens. The sex difference could in part be due to the facts that only residential biological fathers and stepfathers were interviewed, and that among the mothers there are substantial size differences by marital status, with divorced women having larger networks. Had divorced fathers been interviewed, the size differences might have been attenuated. As far as the adolescent networks are concerned, two explanations of the size differences seem reasonable. One possibility is seen in the following account:

> I think probably my dad was hurt when once I just came out and said
> I didn't like Uncle John and I wouldn't go over there anymore—be-
> cause, you know, it's his brother and all, and, like, I should have liked
> him since he was my uncle. (M, 14)

Indeed, several of the adolescents feel that one of the advantages of being older is that they are freer to stop interacting with people they do not particularly care for, such as relatives or friends of the family. Second, while the adolescents' social worlds are expanding somewhat and they are more independent of their parents, they are still restricted to a large extent in their ability to form their own independent, supportive relationships. Thus, adolescents are perhaps in a better position to get rid of some unwelcome network members but are limited in their ability to find replacements.

Adolescents are also more likely than adults to have uniplex rather than multiplex relationships. In one sense this means that there is a greater division of labor between the parts of the adolescent's network. Adults tend to include more people in their networks with whom they have a variety of relationships, for example, colleagues who are also seen socially. In the adolescents' networks there is a strong impression of the interchangeability of members, particularly in the case of age-peers. This, in turn, suggests a greater degree of fluidity in the membership of adolescent networks.

When the adolescents' networks are compared with their parents' networks, there is a moderate degree of overlap. The most overlap occurs in the area of relatives and is most noticeable in the case of the divorced mothers and their children. Only rarely do teens have supportive relationships with relatives who are not included in the parents' networks. This is particularly so following divorce, since divorced mothers rarely include former in-laws in their networks, and adolescents are somewhat less likely to do so. Furthermore, after divorce, adolescents are more likely to include nonrelated adults, a substantial number of whom are friends of the mother.

In comparing parental and adolescent networks, then, several interesting differences emerge. There is some overlap in membership, though not a great deal, indicating that adolescents are at least beginning the process of constructing and maintaining their own support networks. However, it appears that the primary means of doing this is by removing some members, resulting in support networks that are significantly smaller than those of the adults. Presumably, as the teens continue to expand their social worlds—for example, through college and work—they will continue to add new members to their support networks. Furthermore, it is suspected that the relationships will change qualitatively as well, as they develop more multiplex and mutual relationships, characterized by less interchangeability and a higher degree of intimacy.

4

Adolescents and Their Mothers

Despite recent changes in gender roles, women continue to be seen as the primary child rearers in American society. As the parents with the primary responsibility for day-to-day care of the children, mothers are expected to be accessible to meet their children's needs at all times, and women who appear deficient in this area are viewed negatively. In the process of caring for their children, mothers are expected to forge close emotional bonds with them. The relationship, however, may become more problematic when the children become adolescents. At the very least, one would expect the differing perspectives of parents and adolescents to lead to some degree of conflict.

Teenagers and parents face each other from different points in the life cycle, characterized by differing perspectives on time (both past and future), different levels of energy, and different concerns. Adolescence is a time when individuals are attempting to establish an identity and to develop some autonomy and independence from their parents. At the same time, faced with the impending departure of their children from the home and the growing awareness of their own mortality, parents search for evidence that they have been successful in transmitting values and attitudes to their children (Erikson, 1968). Bengtson and Kuypers (1971) argue that, due to their different life cycle perspectives, each group has a "generational stake" in viewing the generation gap in a particular way. Thus, adolescents perceive their attitudes to be more different from their parents than they actually are, in an attempt to maximize their autonomy, and parents perceive their attitudes to be more similar than they actually are, in order to maximize the extent of their value transmission. In this view the most significant generation gap is one in perceptions.

How these differences are played out in the relationships of mothers and their teenage children, and the extent to which their relationships are sensitive to variations in the mother's marital status, are the subjects of Chapter 4. Specifically, the questions addressed are: What role do mothers play in the support networks of their teenage children? In what ways does divorce impact upon the mother-adolescent relationship? How, if at all, does the relationship between a divorced mother and her adolescent child change when she remarries? Is the mother-adolescent relationship affected by the sex or birth order of the teen, or by the presence of more than one child in the family?

MOTHERS AS SUPPORTS

It is clear that mothers are important sources of support for their teens when it is considered that only age-peers are more likely, but only slightly so, to be named as supports. All 30 of the teens name at least one age-peer as a support, whereas all but three name their mothers. Also, one of the three who originally did not include his mother reconsidered later in the interview:

Yeah, thinking about it now, I gotta say my mom is probably a support . . . at least in her own way. She hassles me a lot, but I guess it's stuff she thinks is important for me to be a good person or whatever— grades, stuff like that. Yeah, she hassles me a lot, but she hasn't kicked me out yet, has she? (M, 17)

Significantly, the three adolescents who originally left out their mothers name support networks composed exclusively of age-peers. If the teen names any adults as supportive, the mother is always one of them. In contrast, fathers are named as supports in only a little over half of the networks. Even when both parents are named as supports, the relationships are qualitatively different, as will be seen.

In describing how their mothers are supportive, the adolescents mention a variety of behaviors, including instrumental and emotional aid. All of the teens who see their mothers as supportive include instrumental aid as one type of support received:

My mom really knocks herself out doing stuff for us. I think she cooks about five dinners a night by the time we all get home or have to run off to do something. (F, 16)

There's nothing she doesn't do around here. The cooking, cleaning, wash—if she didn't make my bed, it wouldn't get done. I tell her not to—I don't care if it's not made—but she goes and does it anyway. (M, 16)

Even the teens who do not include their mothers as supports recognize the instrumental aid they provide:

Well, she supports me by buying me clothes and she's the one that does the work so we have an apartment and food and stuff. (F, 15)

The mothers are generally recognized by their adolescent children as investing a considerable amount of time and energy in maintaining the household and providing for the members' needs. This includes cooking, cleaning, and laundry, as well as chauffeuring the teens around and shopping for clothing. This is not very surprising, considering that despite recent sex-role changes, women continue to do the bulk of the housecleaning and child care, even when they are employed full-time (Vanek, 1978). Indeed, over three-quarters of the mothers in the sample are currently employed at least part-time, but they continue to do the bulk of the home and family maintenance chores.

Mothers provide other kinds of support for their teenagers. In part because they are more available than are fathers, mothers often deal with the children's everyday problems. This can include dealing with minor school or friend problems:

There was this math teacher who I thought was really giving me a hard time, and my mom would listen to me gripe all the time, and would kind of help me get through it. (M, 14)

She's good about it, like when one of my friends does something low and I'll be upset or something, she tells me about something like it when she was my age, and it doesn't seem so bad. (F, 13)

At times there is considerable overlap with instrumental aid, since many of the problems encountered by the teens involve access to money or cars:

She's really understanding if I run out of money and something comes up. As long as I tell her what it's for, she almost always comes through. (F, 16)

A good deal of this type of support goes on continually, on a day-to-day basis. One mother, when asked if her son comes to her with his problems, gives the following description:

Sometimes it seems like that's all he does. It starts the minute he comes in the door from school. And when I think about it, that's usually just a continuation of where we left off when he walked out the door in the morning. . . . It's just one thing after another—he needs this or that, money, something for school, new shoes, or he wants the car, or, like today, it's Tuesday and he's already starting in on when he has to be home on Saturday, or he's complaining about something Joey [younger brother] did, or he wants me to ask his father about something. I could go on forever. . . . (mother of 17-year-old son)

In fact, it is not uncommon for mothers to serve as go-betweens for adolescents and fathers. While almost all of the teens from time to time attempt to play one parent against the other, when it is felt that having an ally will strengthen the teen's case in a situation where both parents' approval is required, it is, with only one exception, always the mother who is approached first. Renegotiating an allowance is the most common situation in which the mother's aid is enlisted first. Curfews and, for those old enough to drive, use of the family car are also situations where it is common for the mother's support to be sought first. Reasons for going to the mother first include the following:

It's a little easier for me to talk to my mom, so I'll ask her first and then she talks to my dad. (F, 14)

Well, you know, it sounds kinda bad, but I think my mom understands me better, you know, she knows me a little better, so I think it's easier for her to see what I want. (F, 15)

It seems like every time I ask my dad for something, he just starts in giving me a hard time and we just end up fighting. But I go to my mom for exactly the same thing and it's no big deal, and she usually gets my dad to see it her way. (M, 16)

The role of the mother as go-between or mediator develops in part from the amount of time the mother has spent with the children. Many of the mothers who are currently employed full-time had been full-time mothers when their children were younger. But time and availability are only part of the explanation. There is a division of labor in child care whereby it is seen as the mother's responsibility to deal with the everyday problems of child rearing. One mother explains:

When all three of them were younger, I wasn't working and, well, Bob [husband] was spending incredible hours at the office. He had just been promoted, it was just understood that he didn't want to have to deal with it when he got home . . . oh, you know, the little everyday problems, with one wanting something, or being mad about something. Oh, sure, if it was something important, a problem at school, maybe, I'd talk to him about it. But I guess it just sort of set up a pattern. If there was a problem, I'd hear about it first, and then, depending on how big it was, I'd either take care of it or ask him about it later. (mother of 15-year-old daughter)

In this case the mother serves as a filter, protecting the husband from minor annoyances.

A little over half of the teens in the sample (17) feel that their mothers provide another kind of support—they see them as confidantes. While most of the teens go to their mothers with minor problems or complaints, those whose mothers are confidantes share more. At times this means going to the mother with more serious problems, such as pressure from peers about alcohol or marijuana, or a close girlfriend who thinks she is pregnant. But for the most part it involves a willingness on the part of the teenagers to share their feelings and experiences with the mother, much as they would with a close friend:

Well, it's like I can talk to her about just about anything. Like, I come home from school and I'll sit around and tell her about stuff that happened that day, and it's like she really wants to hear about it. Even though she never met a lot of my teachers and some of the kids I hang with, it's like she knows them because she hears me talk about them a lot. And it's like she's really interested in them. It's funny—I'll tell her about somebody, something they did or something like that, and then I'll forget all about it, and then one day she'll say, "Whatever happened with Lisa?" or whoever, or something like that. (F, 16).

I talk to my mom about all kinds of stuff—girls, if I want to go to college, what I want to do. It's easy. I don't worry about her saying it's bad or getting upset, she just listens. (M, 15)

No, I can't think of anything I wouldn't tell her. I mean, I don't really get into trouble or stuff like that. But even if I did, I think I'd tell her. (F, 13)

Inherent in these descriptions is the notion that the mother will not judge but will listen and perhaps give an opinion. The fact that a substantial number of the teens rely on their mothers as confidantes does not fit the stereotype of teenagers and parents locked in battle, not trusting each other, and communicating little. Indeed, it is interesting that the teens themselves are aware of the stereotype, and feel that perhaps their own relationship with their mother is somewhat unusual:

Well, a lot of the kids I know from school and stuff seem to fight a lot with their parents. And I guess it seems weird sometimes, because I'll say something to someone about telling my mom about something that happened and they'll say, "You told your mom about that?" Like they never would have told theirs. (F, 16)

Sometimes I think it's pretty weird. I'll be saying stuff to her and then I'll think, wait a minute, this is my mom. But it doesn't really seem to matter. (M, 14)

When asked why they think their relationship is different from those of their friends, the adolescents are hard pressed to explain it. Most fall back on some personality trait or characteristic:

She's a good listener. I've heard other people say that about her, too. (F, 13)

I guess that's just the way, you know, the kind of person she is. I just don't think about it. (M, 14)

Others see their mothers as having some kind of experience, or fulfilling another role, that provides her with the necessary skills:

Maybe it's because she's a teacher, so she's around kids all the time and kind of knows where they're coming from. (F, 17)

She's a social worker, and they're supposed to be able to help people with their problems and stuff. (M, 13)

While the mothers might very well differ noticeably in their personal characteristics or skills, there are significant variations in the likelihood of the mother's acting as a confidante related to her marital status. These variations will be discussed later.

The impression received is that the mother-adolescent relationship is characterized by warmth and closeness. This is especially the case when the mother is viewed as a confidante. This does not imply that the relationships are conflict-free. There are three mother-adolescent relationships, in fact, almost wholly characterized by conflict. Typical of this situation is the description from a 15-year-old girl:

Interviewer: How close do you feel to your mother?

Teen: Not really very close. We fight a lot.

Interviewer: What sorts of things do you fight about?

Teen: You name it, we fight about it. Clothes, what I do on the weekends, my grades, how I never do anything around the house to help her.

Interviewer: How do those arguments usually end?

Teen: We just stop talking to each other until we forget about it, or until the next time we fight about something.

Interviewer: Do you talk to her about your problems?

Teen: No. It seems like whenever we start to talk, we just end up arguing, so we don't talk about things very much.

Her mother provides the following account:

I guess I'd have to say that at best it's a stormy relationship. It's been that way for a while. I used to think that if you were open with your kids and treated them like people, you could avoid most problems and have this great relationship. And I am really close to her older sister, so it came as kind of a shock when I thought I was doing all the right things, but here was this child who felt compelled to argue with me about everything—clothes, chores, school, the phone. I thought, OK, she's a different individual, the same rules won't work, but it didn't seem to matter—she wasn't arguing about the rules, she was just arguing. I don't know, I guess it's just her personality. (mother of 15-year-old daughter)

The issues being argued about are not much different from things that most teens argue about with their parents (Douvan and Adelson, 1966). In the sample as a whole, the matters most frequently argued about, in order, are clothes, talking on the telephone, tastes in music, curfews, and grades. Two things, however, distinguish the three conflictual relationships from the others. First, there is very little nonconflictual interaction between the teens and their mothers. When the mothers and teens are not arguing, they are not saying much at all. Second, the arguments themselves are significant in that the issues are never resolved. Satisfactory solutions are not developed; rather, the parties stop talking to one another, thereby cutting off the chance for communication. Furthermore, fights escalate later because unresolved issues usually resurface in subsequent arguments.

There are four cases in which the adolescent and the mother agree that conflict is rare or minimal, and fights or arguments really do not occur. For example:

> *Teen:* Well, I wouldn't say we really argue about stuff. I can't think of the last time we really fought about something. Maybe little things, like cleaning my room. I don't like to do it, and she'll let it go for a while, and then it'll start to get to her and she'll tell me to do it, and I'll complain and maybe I won't do it, and she'll get kind of irritated with me.
>
> *Interviewer:* How are things like that usually resolved? How do you end the argument?
>
> *Teen:* I'll usually end up doing it, because it's hardly ever a big deal. It just takes me a while to get around to it. But that's not really an argument. We don't really argue. If I do something that bothers her, she tells me about it, or I tell her something I don't like, and that's about it. (F, 16)

In this and the other relatively nonconflictual relationships, arguments are largely avoided by dealing with problems or conflicts before they get to the argument stage. When an argument occurs, it almost always ends with an agreeable compromise or one of the parties' accepting the position of the other. It is notable that in the few cases where arguments are rare, there is no discernible pattern of either party's giving in. It does not appear that parents in these instances effectively end the argument by relying on their veto power. While at times this does occur, there are also times when the parent concedes.

The majority of the mother-adolescent relationships fall somewhere between the conflictual and nonconflictual types. In fact, these cases are more accurately represented as two extremes of a continuum rather than as distinct types. Most report that conflict comes and goes. At times the conflict revolves around one particular issue that, whenever it arises, almost inevitably ends in an argument:

> I suppose I'm lucky, considering that for the most part we get along fine. But the one thing we just go around and around about is how often he can go out and when he has to be home. I just don't think that a 16-year-old needs to go out more than one night in a weekend, and despite what "all his friends do," I feel that midnight is too late for him to be out. Well, this has been going on for six months—by midweek he's started making little jabs, trying to make me feel bad about his curfew. By Friday morning he's going full force. We fight about it until he walks out the door Friday night—he always leaves angry—and he doesn't start talking to me again until Sunday. Then we have a couple of days of peace and quiet, and then it starts all over again. (mother of 16-year-old son)

The son says:

> Yeah, we fight. I think she's really unfair about when I gotta be home. It's like she's thinking of when she was my age or something, but it's not the same. I don't think she cares about the time so much, but it's like she just wants to tell me what to do. (M, 16)

Curfews are especially sensitive issues, followed rather closely by driving-related matters, either access to the family car for the teens 16 or over, or, for those teens too young to drive, permission to ride in a car driven by an older teen. There are also conflicts that start with a particular incident which have long-lasting consequences: one involving the return home one night of a 15-year-old girl obviously under the influence of alcohol, and another occurring when a mother accidentally discovers birth control pills in her 16-year-old daughter's purse.

At other times conflict is not related to a particular issue or incident but occurs periodically, seemingly unprovoked, and then stops as quickly as it started. According to one mother:

> I guess that's what living with a teenager is all about. You never know from one day to the next who you're going to be dealing with. One day she's this sensitive, charming girl that's easy to talk to and seems so reasonable, and then the next day it's like I'm right back to the

"terrible two's," complete with temper tantrums. (mother of 15-year-old daughter)

Her daughter describes the situation in similar terms but interprets it differently:

We get along pretty good. Yeah, we fight sometimes. It's like she can't always make up her mind about something . . . well, OK, like letting me go out with my friends in a car—she does, and then it's like she changes her mind, and next time says it's not a good idea, so I can't do it. But then she doesn't understand why I get upset. (F, 15)

Most of the parents in the sample, as well as the adolescents themselves, take much of the conflict in stride. In part this is due to popular stereotypes and the expectations that people have of teenagers and their parents. Those teens who get along well with their mothers sometimes feel they are odd. The mothers, too, take conflict with teenagers as a given. Those mothers whose teens are older—above 15—consider themselves very lucky if they have gotten through the earlier years with a minimum of conflict. Those with younger teens are bracing themselves—or, as the mother of a 13-year-old boy puts it, "I'm holding my breath," waiting for the inevitable storm to hit.

Another reason that parents and adolescents are not very disturbed by the conflict that occurs is that it is only one aspect of their relationship. Even the mother who spends the major part of every week locked in battle over a curfew feels herself to be lucky because outside of that, there are so few problems. The parents and adolescents have disagreements and they argue. But in only three cases does this effectively define the whole of the relationship. The majority of the teens and parents have relationships that include conflict, but also involve caring and communication. Mothers have their share of the day-to-day trials and tribulations of living with adolescents, but in the process of dealing with those problems they build and maintain bonds of warmth and respect with their children. As a 16-year-old girl says, when asked to describe her relationship with her mother, "She's like a friend."

There is evidence that youths and parents perceive each other and their relationship differently, due to the differential stake that each has in the relationship (Bengtson and Kuypers, 1971). There is additional evidence that dyadic agreement between parents and adolescents is influenced by the objectivity and salience of the topic, as well as by social norms (Jessop,

1982). It is assumed that, due to the emotionally intense nature of family relationships and the amount of time spent together, parent-adolescent relationships are salient to both parties. Furthermore, descriptions of and feelings about a relationship are bound to be subjective, even when the reference point is relatively objective, such as "the frequency of conflict." Finally, in American society there are strong norms suggesting that while family members are to love and respect each other, when it comes to teenagers, a good deal of rebellion and conflict is to be expected. It is reasonable, then, to expect parents and adolescents to provide somewhat different descriptions of their relationship.

The first thing that stands out is the extent to which parents and adolescents agree that their relationships are for the most part close and satisfying. In the three conflictual relationships this perception is shared by the mothers and their teens. There are, however, differences in the accounts obtained from the parents and from the adolescents. Some of the differences are a matter of degree, whereas others are qualitative.

One relatively small difference concerns the kinds of support that mothers provide for their teens. The teenagers all recognize the instrumental support provided by mothers in the way of housekeeping, cooking, and other family-maintenance chores. Mothers, on the other hand, tend to downplay the importance of these tasks as support. They recognize that they spend a great deal of time doing them, but they feel that the essence of their support concerns the reasons they do the tasks or the emotional support they provide:

Sure, I do all of that [cooking, cleaning, etc.], and I can't say that I like any of it, but I do it because I love them. I think they know that. (mother of 14-year-old daughter)

I feel real close to my kids—the housecleaning part, well, I think they take that for granted. But they know I'm always there for them. (mother of 13-year-old son)

A second difference involves perceptions of the conflicts that occur. The difference is qualitative—while mothers and teens do not differ much in their estimates of how frequently conflict occurs, they do tend to feel differently about the importance of the conflicts. Mothers tend to see conflicts as having little to do with the issue at hand; rather, they see them as a result of the psychological, and sometimes biological, changes the teenagers are going through:

If it wasn't one thing, it would be another. It doesn't matter what it is—it's just a way of testing me again. (mother of 15-year-old son)

Well, it comes and goes. Sometimes she feels like arguing, and at those times it doesn't matter what I say or do, she'll argue with it. Ten minutes later she's forgotten what it was she was arguing about. (mother of 14-year-old daughter)

This is frustrating for the teens. They do not feel that they are arguing simply for the sake of arguing, nor do they see the issues as inconsequential. One 15-year-old girl recounts the following story:

She wanted to take me shopping for school clothes, I wanted her just to give me what she'd spend and let me do it myself. It was this whole scene—I tried and tried to make her see how I felt, why I wanted to do it. It just turned into a big fight, and I ran to my room and slammed the door, and later she came in, and I was crying, and she said, "Look, I think I've figured out why you're so upset—you're going to start your period in a couple of days, and you know that always makes you oversensitive." She didn't say a thing about anything I had said to her. It's so frustrating. (F, 15)

Of course, not all of the parents respond in this way. Indeed, some of the teens feel from time to time that what they are arguing about is not very important.

The third and largest difference between the teens and their mothers revolves around the mother's role as confidante. While 17 adolescents see their mothers as confidantes, 24 of the mothers see themselves as confidantes and 2 others think they are but are not certain. Obviously it is more difficult for the mothers to answer accurately, because they have no way of knowing whether their children actually confide in them. Most of the mothers assume they do. In part this is wishful thinking. In part it is because most of the teenagers do in fact share some of their problems and feelings with their mothers:

I tell her most stuff, some stuff I don't—No, it's not really the big things I don't tell her, mostly little things. I figure if I take care of it or it works itself out, what's the use of hassling her with it? Well, like, if I get suspended from school, I can't really hide that from her, but if I just get into some little trouble and get detention or something, she doesn't have to find out about that. (M, 17)

The stuff I think would really upset her, I don't say something about. Mostly I leave out the details . . . yeah, sometimes I guess I lie. Like I'm not supposed to be in the car with Michelle [16-year-old friend], so I said her mom brought me home. (F, 15)

For the most part the teenagers censor what they tell their mothers. Because they are being told something, most of the mothers trust that they are hearing complete and accurate stories.

THE EARLY EFFECTS OF DIVORCE

Ten of the mothers in the sample are currently divorced, and the ten remarried women have spent some time living with their children as a divorced mother. All of the mothers have been divorced at least two years, significantly longer for the remarried mothers. Considering this, and the fact that several of the teens were quite young at the time of the divorce, caution is in order when discussing the early effects of divorce on the mother-child relationship. All of the accounts are retrospective, leaving room for errors in memory as well as other distortions that might occur over time. However, it is possible to make some tentative observations about mother-child relationships in the early years following divorce.

Those teenagers who can remember, and all of the mothers, report that the children were initially upset and distressed by the divorce. This seems to have little to do with the quality of the father-child relationship prior to the divorce or with the level of stress and conflict in the home. In part this is because the children were not told much by their parents about the marriage or about the impending divorce, partially as an attempt to shelter them from hostility and conflict:

I didn't think children should see their parents arguing. They were only four and six at the time, and I thought it would just upset them. So they never really knew what was going on. (mother of 13-year-old son)

Others are uncomfortable discussing the matter with their children, unsure of what or how much they should be told:

How do you talk to a 5-year-old about divorce? I wasn't sure I even understood why it had come to that. (mother of 13-year-old son)

Even those parents whose children were older at the time of the divorce had difficulty talking to them about it. The children of this mother were 14 and 17 at the time of the divorce:

> There was always a chance that the divorce wouldn't happen and I didn't want to upset them for nothing. . . . Well, I guess I knew we weren't going to stay together. . . . I was really just afraid to tell them. (mother of 17-year-old son)

In his study of the adjustment to separation, Weiss (1975) finds that many of the children in his sample have been sheltered from the conflicts in their parents' marriages, and thus are unprepared for the possibility of divorce. For the children this means initial shock and confusion:

> I couldn't believe it when my mom told me. I was just . . . so surprised. (F, 15)

> I remember thinking that one of them must have done something really awful . . . well, they didn't fight or anything—they got along fine. (M, 15)

This is especially telling in light of the mother's description of the marriage:

> Are you kidding? Was there conflict in the marriage? Oh, boy, I would say so. We fought about everything, and I mean we fought a lot. In the last two years of the marriage I think we fought every day. It didn't matter what it was about—we just had to fight. . . . Well, we tried, I guess, to keep it from the kids. I mean we didn't fight in front of them, and when he managed to be there for dinner, which wasn't very often, we kept it pretty civil. (mother of 15-year-old son)

Thus, even when conflict does occur, it often takes place after the children are in bed and behind locked doors.

This is not to suggest that the children would necessarily make a smooth adjustment were they more informed about the state of their parents' marriage and the possibility of divorce. While there is evidence that parent-child communication concerning the divorce positively affects adjustment (Jacobson, 1978c), it appears that the majority of children whose parents divorce experience initial distress and anxiety (Weiss, 1975). In their longitudinal study of the impact of divorce, Wallerstein and

Kelly (1974, 1975, 1976) find that almost all children see divorce as a painful and disruptive experience.

The reasons for the children's distress are many and complex. Those discussed here are not meant to be comprehensive. Rather, they are the problems that seem most significant in the accounts of parents and children, and they lead to responses and adjustments that distinguish life in a single-parent home from life in a two-parent home. The first reason for the distress felt by the children and the mothers is tied to the loss of the father. Weiss (1975) reports that even after a painful and conflictual marriage, individuals continue to feel attachment to the ex-spouse and sadness and loneliness upon his/her absence. Many of the mothers and most of the children note that they missed the father a great deal when he left (in only two cases did the mother leave home and obtain the children later):

> For I don't know how long, every time we sat down for supper, I'd start to cry because his chair was empty. (F, 14)

> I called him every single night. My mom didn't know, I said I was calling a friend. I just wanted to talk to him. (M, 17)

There is only a slight relationship between closeness to the father prior to the divorce and the strength of the reaction after his departure. While several of the teens feel relieved that the conflict has ended, or that an abusive or alcoholic parent has left, usually their feelings are mixed. Some of the teens are mourning not only the loss of a parent but also the fact that the parent has not been a different kind of person:

> If only he hadn't drank [sic], I think things would have been a whole lot different. When he's not drinking, he's a great person—he's really fun. If only he hadn't drank [sic]. (M, 17)

Even the teens who had not been very close to their father claim that they miss him, and feel that "things just aren't the same" without him.

In some cases reactions to the loss of the father are exacerbated by other changes. Parental divorce often weakens ties with paternal relatives and strains ties with material kin. If the children have been close to the grandparents, after the divorce they can find themselves deprived of that source of support as well. Furthermore, in over half of the cases, the mother and children moved to a new home during the first year following the separation. In three cases this involved moving into the maternal grandparents' home. In a little over half the cases, the family remained in the same town but moved into a different house or apartment. In the remaining cases the move was to a new geographical location. In some cases the family home was sold as part of the divorce settlement, in some the mother had to find cheaper housing, and in others the move was because of the mother's job or educational plans. In all cases moving is associated with stress and additional loss, including familiar surroundings, neighbors, and friends. Especially in the first year after divorce, loneliness is a pervasive feeling for both the mothers and their children.

Another problem leading to stress and anxiety after divorce has to do with the tremendous amount of responsibility placed upon the mothers. Weiss (1975) suggests that single parents suffer from task, emotional, and responsibility overload. Part of this has to do with the number of things that must be taken care of by one person. Hetherington, Cox, and Cox (1978) note that the main practical problems are related to household maintenance and economic and occupational difficulties. They find that single-parent families eat more fast-food and pickup meals, and the children are likely to have erratic bedtimes and are more often late to school.

The mothers provide a good deal of evidence to support the idea that single parents suffer from overload:

> There was never enough time to do what I had to do. Looking back, I don't know why. Don [ex-husband] had never done anything around the house anyway. But it just seemed like there was so much to do. (mother of 13-year-old daughter)

> I was trying to find a job, buy a car, get a cheaper apartment, worry about paying the bills, deal with lawyers, my ex-husband, my parents, still do the hundreds of things I had always done. (mother of 14-year-old son)

Trying to keep up with the demands is complicated by the fact that the mothers are also trying to cope with their distress and anxiety:

> I must have been frantic at the time. I couldn't stand to be still, so I was all the time doing something. The problem was, it didn't always make sense. I remember, one day not long after the divorce the kids left for school and I decided to clean the basement. I went through boxes, threw stuff out, cleaned everything. I never stopped—I even washed the walls. The next thing I know, the kids are coming in the

door from school. I had forgotten to eat lunch, I had started nothing for their supper, but I had the cleanest basement in town. (mother of 13-year-old son)

Besides the instrumental tasks that have to be done, mothers have to deal with the emotional needs of their children, and have almost full responsibility for decisions pertaining to them. On the whole, mothers are sensitive to their children's distress and their needs for increased attention and support. About half of the divorced mothers say they deal with this by being "softer" on the children—not disciplining them as harshly, giving in to them on such things as later bedtimes or the food they eat, or by doing special things for them:

I felt those kids had really been through a lot, and I just didn't want to make it any harder on them. I figured they'd lost a father, and if I came down hard on them, they'd feel like they'd lost me, too. (mother of 14-year-old daughter)

The other half of the mothers feel that the best thing they can do for their children is to keep things as close to normal as possible, and sometimes to be stricter than they were prior to the divorce:

I thought it was really important that they knew I had things under control. That meant they weren't going to get away with murder and things were going to pretty much stay the same. (mother of 15-year-old daughter)

Virtually all of the mothers feel they have to make some adjustments in enforcing their authority and disciplining the children, although over half feel that prior to the divorce this had been their responsibility anyway:

It's kind of funny thinking about it now, but before the divorce I was the one who was expected to keep the kids in line. I made the decisions and doled out the punishments. But I guess in a way I used him [ex-husband] as a threat—sort of more "Wait till your father gets home" or "If you don't like my punishment, your father's will be ten times worse." And he very rarely had to do anything—it was just that threat. So when he left, the rules and punishments and things stayed the same, and I was still doing them, but now I had to convince the kids to do it for me, and not because they were afraid of their father. (mother of 14-year-old daughter)

In this case the father has served as a symbolic authority figure more than a real one, a finding noted by others (Weiss, 1975). When this symbol was removed, several mothers found that they had to reassert their authority, without the father's backup.

A third problem faced by the mothers and children following divorce is economic. On the average, men's economic position improves following divorce, while that of women worsens (Brandwein et al., 1974). Wallerstein and Kelly (1979) find that even in middle-class families, mothers and their children experience a significant decline in their standard of living that occurs relatively rapidly following separation. All of the mothers claim they are worse off economically after the divorce. Those women who had not been employed have to find work, often after many years out of the labor force and with few marketable skills. Even the employed women find themselves at a disadvantage, in part because they have custody of the children and in part because their jobs pay less than their husbands'. Thus, mothers find themselves worrying about money and attempting to cut corners while still meeting the needs of their children.

A fourth and related problem is a very restricted social life on the part of the mothers:

> That first year I don't think I had a minute to myself, there was always something that had to be done. Besides, who could afford a sitter? (mother of 15-year-old son)

The statement of this mother highlights one of the largest restrictions faced—that of the children. Because the mothers have custody of the children, they cannot just take some time off and go shopping or to a movie. There is the practical problem of having to arrange for a baby-sitter, and the financial problem of paying one. But there is more to it than that:

> I don't know, I was working all day, doing all of the housework at night, and I had no adult friends. I really needed to get out of the house and away from the kids. But as it was, they didn't see much of me. Leaving them with a sitter just didn't seem like a good idea. (mother of 13-year-old son)

Because they feel their children are anxious and vulnerable, mothers hesitate to go out and enjoy themselves, even for a few hours every several weeks, if it means leaving the children with a baby-sitter. Thus, there is an element of guilt in the discussions of the mothers.

Despite the many problems faced, all of the mothers, and those children who can remember, feel that the situation has improved tremendously. In some cases this is because one or more of the problems has gone away—for instance, the mother finishes her education or gets a good job that relieves the financial concerns. In the majority of cases, however, the problems do not go away; rather, the families adapt and adjust to them. Other research has found that, on the average, the adjustment to divorce takes two to three years (Ambert, 1984; Hetherington et al., 1978). For the most part, mothers report that the major problems have been worked out and things once again are running smoothly within a few years of the divorce. While each family copes with the divorce in slightly different ways, there are discernible patterns in the ways divorced mothers and their children adjust, and it is often these patterns that distinguish single-parent homes from two-parent homes.

LIFE IN A SINGLE-PARENT HOME

There are two patterns in the families that are responses to the problems of overload and limited economic resources. One pattern concerns the authority hierarchy in the household. After the divorce there is a good deal more negotiation between mother and children concerning responsibilities and decisions. This is partially due to the loss of the father as backup authority figure and the fact that several of the children reportedly take advantage of the situation by repeatedly testing the mother. In addition, because several of the mothers have had to return to work and have other things to worry about, they cannot closely oversee their children. Thus, they have to rely on their children to take more responsibility for themselves. This proves to be somewhat easier when the children are allowed to voice their opinions and have a say in the decision:

> I hate to admit it, but for over a year my kids were "latch-key children." I didn't get home until almost 6:00 and I just couldn't pay a sitter. Well, they had to take certain responsibilities so that they were safe and nothing terrible would happen. And since Amy was only 8 then, I had to rely on Susan (then 10) to take care of her. While obviously I had to set some rules—no cooking, no people in the house—the whole arrangement worked better when I let Susan make some of the decisions—like having a friend over once in a while after school, or getting snacks for her and Amy. (mother of 15-year-old daughter)

At times the constant negotiations can be trying. In his research on separation, Weiss (1975) finds that the levels of what is appropriate for and expected of adults and children are far less distinct in single-parent homes than they are in two-parent homes. There is evidence of that blurred distinction here as well:

> Sometimes it was crazy. I'd find myself in the middle of endless discussions of why he should or shouldn't be able to do something, or why I was being unfair, and I'd think, hey, wait a minute—he's talking to me like he's an adult, but he's just a 12-year-old child! (mother of 15-year-old son)

Several of the adolescents feel that they are getting a greater say in household matters, and feel it is justified:

> It just seems fair. If I'm going to give up stuff after school so I can baby-sit and start dinner and stuff, then I think I should be able to say how I feel about things, you know, be treated like, well, I guess an adult. (F, 14)

While it is difficult and tiring to have to negotiate with one's children, most of the mothers feel that the advantages outweigh the disadvantages and that the children benefit from having to present their case and take responsibility for decisions.

Increased negotiation between mother and children is also promoted by the fact that the children are often presented with different rules and responsibilities when with their fathers. Most of the children have some continued contact with their noncustodial father, and this can lead to problems:

> When we were living together, he was perfectly happy to let me set all the rules and watch over what they were doing. But then he moves out and all of a sudden decides that my rules aren't any good—I'm too strict, or I let them get away with too much. So of course they come home and say, "Dad says you should let us stay up later." (mother of 16-year-old daughter)

Several of the mothers note that they fight more with their husbands about child-related matters since the divorce than they did before. Some deal with this by drawing a clear line between the two households, and expecting the children to move back and forth between two different sets of rules. For the most part the children handle this relatively well, with only minor difficulties:

> It's not a big deal—they're two different people, so they do things differently. I mean, there's always stuff you do in some places and in others it's not OK, or you act differently with different people. (M, 16)

This comment is especially interesting because there is some evidence suggesting that adolescents living with both parents do not make clear distinctions between their mothers and their fathers in their perceptions of their parents' attitudes (Acock and Bengtson, 1980), or in their estimates of how much they like each parent (Acock et al., 1982).

Another response of several mothers to rule conflicts with the father is to draw him into negotiations to reach a compromise. Many times this is a very complex process in which both parents, acting independently, as well as at least one child, have a say in the decision being made. It is this complexity in the decision-making process that in part distinguishes single-parent families from two-parent families.

A second outcome stemming from the single mother's overload and limited financial resources is that virtually all of the children in single-mother households are expected to share in the running and maintenance of the household. All of the mothers rely upon their children to do far more than had they not divorced. This includes even the younger children and extends to such things as cooking and doing the laundry. One mother has taken her 15-year-old daughter with her to a car-maintenance course at a community college because she will soon be learning to drive and can then help the mother with simple upkeep on the family car. The degree to which the tasks and responsibilities are organized is striking. Four of the ten families have elaborate charts drawn up (always taped to the refrigerator) outlining who is to do what, and when the tasks are to be rotated. Most of the others report that they have given much thought to the division of labor and often renegotiate and redistribute tasks:

> Before the divorce I just did it all. Oh, there were certain things I did on certain days, but for the most part I did it when I wanted to or when something needed doing. After the divorce, and I was working, the kids had to do a lot. I don't get home till after 5:30, so they have to start dinner. They put in loads of clothes, and really do a lot of the cleaning. Since I'm not here, I have to trust them to do it, and the

more clearly it's laid out, the more likely it is it'll get done. . . . The little ones can't do as much, and I want to be fair, so there's a lot of working in pairs, and trading off every week, things like that. Figuring all of this out sometimes takes more time than actually doing it. (mother of 14-year-old son)

Most of the adolescents, while sometimes finding the added responsibility to be burdensome, see it as necessary:

Sometimes I'll get upset because my friends want to do something but I have to be home when Shelley [younger sister] gets home from school, or I have to start dinner. But I know I have to do it. (F, 15)

We're a team—that's what my mom always says, and it's true. We gotta work together. Sure, it's a pain sometimes, but everybody has to do their part. It's just the way it is. (M, 13)

This spirit of teamwork distinguishes the single-parent homes from the two-parent homes. The adolescents in the two-parent families have chores, but they do not do as many, and doing them is usually tied to a concrete reward, such as an allowance or being able to go out on weekends.

The sex-typing of chores also distinguishes the married and divorced families. In the two-parent families there is a clear division in the chores assigned on the basis of sex. Both boys and girls have responsibility for cleaning their rooms. Girls are most likely to have kitchen-related chores, especially clearing and washing dishes, and other housecleaning tasks, such as vacuuming and, occasionally, cleaning the bathroom. Boys often take out the garbage, and are likely to be expected to mow the lawn and do related tasks, such as cleaning the garage. When boys have other chores, the most common is doing the dishes. This sex-based division of labor breaks down in the one-parent families. As one mother explains:

I think it's important that boys know how to do those things, like cooking, cleaning. After we separated, my ex-husband moved back in with his parents! He said to save money, but I bet you anything the biggest reason was he didn't know how to heat a can of soup, and he couldn't have done his laundry if his life depended on it. Well, Kurt [16-year-old son] isn't going to grow up like that. (mother of 16-year-old son)

While this is probably an exaggeration, it is a sentiment widely expressed by the divorced mothers. Perhaps because of their own traditional experiences prior to the divorce and their movement into more nontraditional areas afterward—such as car maintenance, budgeting, yard work, and home repairs—they see the advantages of flexibility and having a broad repertoire of skills and experiences.

A third distinct pattern in divorced families is related to the absence of another adult from the home and the loneliness experienced by the mothers. In a study of joint custody, Leupnitz (1982) finds that almost two-thirds of the custodial mothers and fathers who interviewed report that there is no overlap between their support groups pre- and post-divorce. This is largely because before the divorce the spouse is the support network, a finding supported here. All of the married persons name their spouse as their primary source of support, and about half say there is really no one else they rely upon for support. Under these circumstances divorce results in the loss of a major, if not the sole, source of support. While lack of support and social isolation may be less of a problem for working women (Hetherington et al., 1978), there are practical limitations on the ability of divorced mothers to socialize, due to the constraints of children and money.

One seemingly common response to this problem is for divorced mothers to rely on their children for support. While none of the women in intact marriages name their children as supports, seven of the mothers currently divorced name the target child as a support and two others name a child who is not in the sample (one is away at college, the other is living in his own apartment). According to one mother,

My daughter is my best friend. I can't wait till she gets home from school. . . . We just talk about whatever. . . . Well, I don't know, I always wanted to be close to her, and wanted to make a real effort to be open with her and close to her—my mother wasn't really like that. So I'd like to think we'd be this close even if we hadn't divorced. I mean, it's kind of ironic if you have to get a divorce to be close to your kids. But I can see how it's easier. If he were here, I guess I'd be talking to him more instead, but I also don't think I'd feel as free to talk to her about some things . . . oh, like sex, or how I felt about the marriage. (mother of 15-year-old daughter)

One adolescent explains:

She's like a friend. I guess that's it, really. Because she tells me stuff about her, too. It's not really like I just tell her all the stuff that goes on with me and she just sits there and listens. I mean, she does that, but she talks to me about her problems and stuff, too. (F, 16)

It is this two-way interaction that distinguishes divorced mother-adolescent relationships from married mother-adolescent relationships. While married mothers can act as confidantes for their children, they never rely on their children to fill this role. Divorced mothers, however, are as likely to confide in their children as their children are to confide in them.

The final distinguishing aspect of divorced-mother families is closely related to restricted social lives and tight finances, exacerbated by guilt over leaving the children with baby-sitters. In the first year or two after divorce the mothers deal with these problems by having virtually no social life. Once the adjustment to divorce has proceeded, and especially once the women begin meeting new people at work or school, it becomes more difficult to stay home. A rather common response is to incorporate the children into their social lives. Over half of the divorced mothers often take their children to social events or other activities that they probably would not take them to under ordinary circumstances:

I was working as a secretary then in a pretty large office and it was sort of a custom for all the girls in the office to go out every other week on payday for a drink and then dinner. At first I didn't go, because of Josh and Jamie [then nine and six], and finally one of the girls said I should just bring them along. I felt kind of funny, but it was either that or I didn't go. So I took them, and it was fine. They kept each other company, they got to go out, I gave them quarters for the video games, and it was still cheaper than a sitter. (mother of 13-year-old son)

At first, when I went back to graduate school, I tried doing everything I could during the day and then late at night when the kids had gone to bed. But it just didn't work. I wasn't getting everything done, and besides, I was missing out on things like group discussions and people getting together to study for exams. So I just started packing them up after dinner and taking them back with me. I felt kind of guilty sometimes, but they actually seemed to think it was kind of an adventure. They'd take their homework and some games and a radio, and they really got a lot of attention from my friends. Sometimes we'd all go out for pizza or hamburgers. Once in a while, not very often, if I had a big exam, or a paper to finish, they'd take sleeping bags and go to sleep on the floor of my office. (mother of 14-year-old daughter)

While less common, a few of the divorced mothers sometimes take their children along on dates:

A couple of years ago I was dating a guy from work, but I felt bad about leaving the kids, and the sitter was expensive, so we didn't go out as often as we'd like, so we worked it out that maybe once a week, maybe not that much, we took the kids along. The best thing to do was to take them to the drive-in. They'd wear their pajamas and we'd get them some popcorn and they'd be asleep in half an hour or so. (mother of 14-year-old daughter)

Seldom are children in married households integrated into their parents' social lives, unless the activity is a family outing or a child-centered activity. Thus, children living with divorced mothers are exposed to a variety of contacts with adults, under circumstances not likely to occur had their parents been married.

Clearly, divorced-mother households are distinguished from two-parent households in that there is more negotiation in the decision-making process, children have more responsibilities in the household, they are commonly relied upon by their mothers as sources of support and as confidants, and they are often exposed to nonrelated adults and to adult social situations at relatively early ages. The question that naturally arises is whether this is good for children. How much responsibility is too much for children? Should parents confide in their children? Is it good for children to participate in adult activities? These and related questions have often been raised by researchers concerned with the impact of divorce on children.

One concern relating to the increased responsibility and participation in adult activities is that of "premature maturity," whereby the teen relinquishes age-appropriate interests for adult interests (Weiss, 1975). In American society the norm is to encourage children to be children, protecting them from growing up too soon. A related concern revolves around the closeness of the mother-child relationship after divorce. This has been of most concern to psychoanalysts and other practitioners (Fast and Cain, 1966; Messinger, 1976; Neubauer, 1960; Visher and Visher, 1979). In their article "When Parent Becomes Peer," Glenwick and Mowrey (1986) suggest that mothers in these cases are no longer fulfilling the role requirements of mother, but are relating to their children as peers, a situation exacerbated by relative isolation. From these perspectives the close mother-child bond is pathological, and the clinical goal is to reestablish appropriate boundaries between parent and child.

It is quite clear that the mother-adolescent relationship is different when the mother is divorced. Whether it is good, bad, or pathological is a more complex question and, on the basis of these data, one that can be answered in only a limited way. The teenager's adjustment or psychological well-being is not assessed using standard psychological instruments. However, on the basis of the discussions with the teens there is very little, if any, evidence that they are being harmed by the increased responsibility or the greater closeness of the relationship with their mothers. This is not to say that the situation is all good, or that the adolescents see no disadvantages in the situation. There is, in fact, a good deal of ambivalence expressed:

Yeah, I get tired of all the stuff I have to do. I see my friends, and their parents don't expect them to do much—they can come and go. And I think it's not fair sometimes. But then, in a way, I think they're kind of spoiled, too, and I think it's probably good that I do the stuff I do. (F, 14)

There are times when I get kind of tired listening to my mom's problems. I don't mean she does it all the time or anything like that. It's just sometimes I'll think, "Look, you're the mother, you should be able to figure this all out." But then I think, she listens to me go on all the time about stuff, and it's really just the same thing. I get tired of listening to my friends sometimes, too. But that's the way it is; if someone's your friend, you listen to them and they listen to you. (F, 15)

Thus, it is the reciprocity of the relationship that stands out. In a way, the adolescents in these situations are getting a fuller, more complex, and perhaps more realistic perspective on family living and relationships. They not only receive from the family, they give to it, thus being exposed to the burdens as well as the benefits of living in a family. They see their mothers as strong and capable in some situations and as in need of support in others, as being good listeners at the same time that they need someone to listen to them.

In part because of biases regarding one-parent families, researchers have rarely considered the possibility of benefits from the close mother-child relationship. One exception is the suggestion that the verbal skills of children in single-parent homes may be enhanced by their close relationship with their mothers and their increased responsibilities in household management (Nelson and Maccoby, 1967). There is informal evidence of this in the conversations with the adolescents. Overall, adolescents living with a divorced mother are more articulate, have fewer difficulties answering questions, are more comfortable with the interview situation, and generally seem more mature in their responses.

At the same time that there may be advantages to living with a single parent, it is important to be cautious about these findings. There might very well be circumstances under which living with a single parent can have negative effects. The adolescents in this sample do not come from a clinical population. While a few have seen a counselor at one time or another, all of the adolescents appear to be functioning well, with few problems at home or at school. However, the teens also do not comprise a random sample. All are white and middle-class, and come from families where the parents are relatively well educated.

Perhaps crucial in understanding the positive outcomes is the fact that, in general, these teenagers do not relinquish age-appropriate activities, nor do they have an exceptionally close relationship with only their mothers. Rather, their increased home responsibilities are balanced by their other interests and activities, and the friendship with their mother is only one of a number of supportive relationships they have with other people. This is true as well of the mothers—they rely on other adults as well as on their children for support. On the average, the support networks of the divorced mothers are larger than those of the married or remarried mothers. In cases where the family is socially isolated, or where the mother is incapable of relying upon herself or other adults, a pathological situation may develop. It does not appear, however, that this is an inevitable consequence of living with a single parent.

REMARRIAGE AND THE MOTHER-ADOLESCENT RELATIONSHIP

For many children, living with a divorced mother is a temporary state until she remarries. While the mother-child relationship changes and takes on particular characteristics following divorce, it is expected that the relationship will change further upon the mother's remarriage. The vast majority of the research literature on children and remarriage either has centered upon the stepchild-stepparent relationship exclusively (see, e.g., Ganong and Coleman, 1984; Robinson, 1984) or has considered the impacts of children on the relationship of remarried couples (Duberman, 1975; Furstenberg and Spanier, 1984). Clearly, the stepchild-stepparent relationship is important for the functioning and well-being of the entire family. What has seldom been considered is the impact of a stepparent in the home on the divorced mother-adolescent relationship.

The close divorced mother-adolescent relationship, which in some ways resembles a friendship more than a mother-child relationship, conflicts with the primacy of the marital relationship within families. In most first marriages the couple relationship is established and developed before children enter the constellation (Furstenberg and Spanier, 1984). In remarriages where children from previous marriages are present, the new spouse comes into a situation where, first of all, the couple identity has not been established prior to having children and, second, where the parent-child relationship has had primacy due to the experience of adjusting to the divorce. This situation significantly affects the mother-child relationship as well as the stepparent-stepchild relationship.

Respondents living in remarried households were asked how their relationships have changed since the remarriage. Generally, the mothers see the marital relationship as being primary:

> It would only cause trouble if I kept putting my kids ahead of him. That's not right. Sure, they're my kids, but he's my husband now, and that comes first. (mother of 15-year-old son)

Most mothers share this view, although they clearly are sensitive to the difficulties this causes for the children:

> It was hard on Brian [15-year-old] when I married again. He was used to having me all to himself, and I think I did whatever I could to make the change easier for him, but things couldn't stay the same. If his father and I had stayed married, it would have been the same—he wouldn't have had all my attention. He just had to understand that. (mother of 15-year-old son)

The children do understand, but for most the transition is not an easy one. While some seem to accept the stepfather easily, many have mixed emotions:

> I guess I was jealous. Sure, I know they're married and that's the way it was supposed to be, but I didn't like it. (F, 16)

Jealousy is a common reaction, and several of the adolescents admit that they have actively tried to come between their mother and their stepfather:

> It's kind of embarrassing. I was a real brat. All I ever did was

complain to my mom about what a jerk he was and how much I hated him. You know, it wasn't really true, but I was so mad. (M, 14)

I was pretty sneaky. I didn't let them have any time alone. I was always there. It must have driven them crazy. I just wasn't ready to share her with anyone. (F, 15)

These problems are usually worked out, but in the beginning, establishing the marital relationship as primary is difficult, at best.

While putting the marriage first is the majority response, three of the mothers follow different strategies. Two attempt to treat each of the relationships equally. One of these is a very complex situation in which both spouses have children from previous marriages:

Well, it became clear very early on that this was a very complicated thing and the problems weren't going to be solved with any easy solution. I mean, can you imagine? We had six teenagers in the house at the same time! It took a while, but what we did was to try to set up everyone as equally important as everybody else. Tom and I had time alone, and we each spent time alone with our own kids. There were some things it was agreed that they'd go to their own parent for, but anything that affected the family, or conflicted with the other's rules, was a family matter that was settled by all of us. (mother of 17-year-old daughter)

One mother has established her relationship with her children as the primary one, but not without difficulties:

Me and the kids had been on our own for almost six years. That's a long time—a lot of patterns and things get established and it's hard, and I don't even know if it's fair to try and change them. After all, they're the only kids I'll ever have, and no one will come between us. . . . Yeah, it has caused some problems, but I was clear on this right from the start—I wanted to be with him and marry him, but no one would come between my kids and me. (mother of 14-year-old daughter)

As a result of the establishment of the new spousal relationship, the mother-adolescent relationship undergoes various changes. Remarried mothers are more likely than married mothers, but less likely than divorced mothers, to confide in their children. The same pattern applies to adolescents confiding in their mothers. This is probably the most significant change identified by the adolescents and mothers:

> We don't talk as much anymore. Oh, about some stuff we do—what's goin' on at school. But we don't just sit around and make popcorn and talk like we used to. (F, 15)

> There's not as much time, you know, to just be together and fool around and talk. (F, 13)

> I don't think it would be right to talk to him the way I used to. He understands. (mother of 15-year-old son)

To some extent the son does understand, although he is not entirely happy with the situation, even three years after the remarriage:

> We don't talk as much. I mean, I know why. . . . Well, like Jack's there now, and they talk about stuff, so I guess it wouldn't be right, but it's like I still feel like she doesn't need me anymore, so I don't like that. (M, 15)

Even when the confidante role continues, there are recognizable differences:

> I very much wanted to be close to her and keep things as much as possible like they were before. But at the same time it wouldn't be fair to Steve [husband] if I told Deanna [16-year-old daughter] things about him in confidence. So we just had to draw some boundaries. (mother of 16-year-old daughter)

> Yeah, some things changed. Well, we still talk a lot, but it's kind of different. Like, I can talk to her about David [stepfather], but it's not like she'll just sit there and listen to me run him down. But if I have a problem with him, she'll listen, and maybe say, "Well, why don't you try this . . . ," or she'll try to explain to me why he does something. (M, 15)

Thus, after remarriage, adjustments are made in the mother-adolescent relationship. Usually early efforts are made to establish the primacy of the spousal relationship, which affects the nature of the mother-adolescent relationship.

While living in divorced households, most of the teens have established very close relationships with their mothers, making the remarriage transition a difficult one. At the same time the adolescents have benefited from their experiences living with a divorced mother. When asked what they most like about their children, the remarried mothers are as likely as the divorced mothers to value their independence and sensitivity to others— they are good listeners or work well with others. Among other things, this means that the adolescents have supportive relationships outside the family, and are able to establish their own friendships and independent interests and activities. Indeed, several of the adolescents in remarried families stand out because of their supportive ties with nonfamily adults.

GENDER, AGE, AND THE ADOLESCENT-MOTHER RELATIONSHIP

While variations in the mother-adolescent relationship by family type are quite distinct, gender and age also have an effect although, overall, the differences are small. Older adolescents, about 15 and older, and girls are somewhat more likely to discuss problems with their mothers and to feel closer to them. Teens also describe having more common interests with the same-sex parent, not a surprising finding, given the persistence of gender-based socialization patterns. However, when the adolescent's gender and parents' marital status are considered jointly, it becomes apparent that the largest differences between males and females in relationships with mothers are seen among the teens in intact families. Among adolescents living with a divorced mother, gender differences are quite small, and they are only slightly larger among those living in stepfamilies.

At first it seems somewhat surprising that males and females are so similar in their relationships with their mothers. However, it is possible that divorce diminishes some of the constraints usually placed on the mother-adolescent relationship by the age or sex of the child. Why this is the case is not altogether clear, although some speculations can be advanced. In intact families, adolescents are segregated from their parents along gender and, especially, age lines. When the parents divorce, both of these lines can become blurred. In the areas of authority and discipline, there is much more open negotiation in divorced households, with a tendency for mothers and children to approach each other on more equal footing. Thus, at least one of the barriers between mothers and children breaks down.

Furthermore, boys in divorced households may be particularly affected by the decreased sex-typing of activities and responsibilities in divorced households. This is hinted at in the early father-absence literature when it is suggested that boys living with their mother are less likely to take on appropriate masculine traits and behaviors (Longfellow, 1979). While a good deal of effort has been made to show that mothers can reinforce masculine behaviors, and that males besides the father can act as masculine role models, in light of increased attention to negative consequences of gender stereotyping, it can be argued that males, in particular, benefit from the more egalitarian division of labor in divorced households. They may gain experience and flexibility, and at the very least they are in a better position to develop a close relationship with their mothers.

CONCLUSIONS

Despite the negative press given to relationships between parents and their teenagers, the overwhelming conclusion here is that the mother-adolescent relationship is a strong and supportive one. Conflicts and differences of opinion arise, sometimes frequently, but they occur in the context of a relationship that is multifaceted. It is characterized by warmth and mutual enjoyment as well as by conflict. What many researchers have failed to recognize is that people, including parents and teenagers, can disagree, even strongly, yet still love and respect each other.

What clearly distinguishes the divorced mother-adolescent relationship is its mutuality and reciprocity. Not only do the teenagers seek support from and confide in their mothers, but the mothers seek support from and confide in their children. Despite the concerns of counselors and psycho-analysts, this close and supportive relationship does not appear to be overly problematic for the teenagers; rather, they seem to benefit by way of increased maturity, communication skills, and independence. While an overly close mother-child relationship after divorce has the potential to be harmful, this is not a necessary or inevitable outcome. Future research should carefully assess the impact of extenuating circumstances on the divorced mother-adolescent relationship. Where both the adolescent and the mother have other supportive relationships, and are involved in their own interests and activities, the close bond between them will likely be less harmful, and perhaps more beneficial, than in the case where they are socially isolated and have few, if any, additional supports.

The remarriage situation is a complex one for the mother-adolescent relationship. On the one hand, they have spent several years together as a single-parent family and in the process have established an especially close and supportive relationship. On the other hand, in American society the spousal relationship is recognized as primary. When a new spouse enters the picture, it can be a stressful and conflictual transition, with jealousy and resentment likely to be the initial reactions. The aspect of the mother-adolescent relationship that is most likely to change is the adolescent's role as confidant. Remarried mothers are less likely than divorced mothers, but more likely than married mothers, to confide in their children. Furthermore, even when the confiding continues, rarely does it extend to the topic of the stepfather or the marriage.

When discussing parent-adolescent relationships, it is important to view the family as an interacting system of relations. The mother-adolescent relationship is affected by the characteristics of the individuals involved, as well as by the structural aspects of the presence of a father or stepfather. This complex set of relations is expected to change over time and to have implications for the well-being of everyone concerned.

5

Adolescents and Their Fathers

It has become fashionable in recent years to talk about the breakdown of traditional sex roles and the impact of this change on men and women, including the assumed increasing interest on the part of men in fathering. In the popular culture this is seen on television and in movies such as *Kramer vs. Kramer*, *Mr. Mom*, and *Three Men and a Baby*. It is reflected as well in the rediscovery of fathers by social scientists. Fein (1978) has traced the changes in social scientific views on fathers through three phases. In the traditional perspective the father fulfills his role by being a good provider and an authority figure. With the modern perspective comes a focus on the vulnerability of children and the hazards of growing up without a father. The newest view, the emergent perspective, is androgynous in assuming that men are no less able to be nurturant and involved with their children than are women.

New perspectives have led to new questions and new research. For many decades little was known about the ways fathers and children interact with each other, and the impact of this interaction on both parties. The fact that fathers are left out of a good deal of child development research has as much to do with views on mothers as it does with views on fathers. The assumption is that the mother is the primary parent and nurturer, and therefore has the most direct and significant effect on the children (Parke, 1981). With the rediscovery of fathers and the focus on their nurturing abilities comes research that looks at fathers and children, beginning with pregnancy. Thus, some researchers have considered the changes that men go through during their partners' pregnancies (Bittman and Zalk, 1978;

Liebenberg, 1967), while others have considered the impact of the father's presence during labor and delivery (Hennenborn and Cogan, 1975).

While it is encouraging to know that men can be nurturant toward their children and involved in their families, little research has addressed the question of how many men actually are involved and nurturant. In the first place, there is evidence that a decreasing proportion of men's adult lives is spent in environments where there are children (Eggebeen and Uhlenburg, 1985). Second, time budget studies (Meissner et al., 1975; J. Robinson, 1977; Walker and Woods, 1976) have consistently found that the amount of family work (housework and child care) performed by husbands is quite small, that husbands do significantly less than wives, and that there are no significant differences between husbands whose wives are employed outside the home and those whose wives are not. It appears that there is a fairly large difference between what men can do in theory and what they do in practice.

More careful attention needs to be paid to the actual interaction between fathers and children in a family system context. Father-child interaction is likely to affect, and to be affected by, mother-child interaction. As a step in this direction the father-adolescent relationship can be explored by comparing it with the mother-adolescent relationship and by considering variations in the relationship related to the father's marital status. Specifically, questions to be addressed include the following: What role, if any, do fathers play in the support networks of their adolescent children? How is the father-adolescent relationship similar to and different from the mother-adolescent relationship? Do divorced fathers differ from non-divorced fathers in their relationships with their children? Do stepfathers differ from custodial and noncustodial biological fathers in their relationships with their children? Does the presence of a stepfather affect the relationship between the noncustodial father and his children?

FATHERS IN ADOLESCENT SUPPORT NETWORKS

The first thing that stands out concerning fathers and their adolescent children is the frequency with which fathers are left out of their children's networks. Just a little over half of the biological fathers are seen as supports, compared with all but three of the mothers. Furthermore, several of these fathers were not listed in the initial description of the support network and were included only after further consideration:

Oh, well, sure, my dad is a support. I mean, it's important that he's here. It's just that, well, like when you say, "Who are the people that support you?" I guess I just think of it more as, just, like, I don't know, somebody that does stuff a lot, every day or something. (M, 16)

It should be remembered that all of the teens are living with their mothers, whereas only ten are living with their biological fathers. However, when teens in the three family types are compared, the differences are quite small. Seven of the teens in married families see their father as a support, compared with five teens living with a divorced mother and five living with a remarried mother. It appears that a common residence is neither a guarantee nor a requirement for a supportive relationship between fathers and their teenage children.

It is also significant that fathers and teens have difficulty qualitatively describing their relationships. Since only fathers living with their teens were interviewed, and one such father was unable to schedule a convenient interview time, only nine fathers were interviewed. However, when the accounts of fathers and adolescents, as well as of mothers, are considered, several patterns emerge.

Most of the respondents recognize the father as an authority figure in the family, although in many cases it is a role that very seldom is exercised:

> He sets my rules, him and my mom. . . . Well, I guess they both do it, but it seems that she checks stuff out with him, but I don't think he checks it out with her. (M, 14)

> I know that when I get into real trouble, he's the one that'll do something about it, you know, punish me. It's not real often. (M, 13)

Even when the father has the final say, decisions are usually carried out by the mother:

> My mom and dad both talk about it, they're both important, I guess. I think my dad usually decides if they don't agree. I think, I'm not real sure about that, but then it's almost always my mom who'll come and tell me what they decided. (F, 15)

This arrangement decreases the likelihood that the adolescents will negotiate directly with their fathers, and it means that often fathers do not have to deal with the frustrations of enforcing the rules and regulations:

> I have to admit, sometimes I feel like I'm really getting dumped on. Even if we both agree on a decision, if it's something the kids aren't

going to like, I'm going to be the one that hears about it—all the flak comes down on me, because they won't do that to him. I guess they know better. (mother of 17-year-old daughter)

Fathers touch on a related theme:

I think I'm important to them. I'm there . . . you know, they look at me and see what I've done. I think I've encouraged them to work hard and do things well. Like, my own father, when I was growing up, he didn't do a lot of things with me, and I'm sure I didn't appreciate it at the time, but looking back I see how important he was. He really pushed me, and I always wanted to please him. (father of 15-year-old son)

It's very important for kids to have a father they can look up to. Someone that shows them it's important to do your best. That's what fathers are supposed to do. (father of 15-year-old daughter)

Few teens recognize their fathers as achievement motivators, and generally fathers acknowledge that their children probably do not appreciate them as such, although they express the hope that their children will, as they get older. Interestingly, in attempting to describe their roles as fathers, men are as likely to draw on their relationships with their own fathers as on their relationships with their children.

There is a more concrete aspect of the father's role that affords more immediate pleasure to fathers and teens and, indirectly, to mothers. Over half of the resident fathers and teens have relatively frequent and regular leisure or social activities that they share. Several other fathers attempt to spend some enjoyable time with their children, although work and school schedules sometimes make it difficult:

Whenever there's something decent around and I think it's something I could sit through, I like to take them to the movies on Sunday afternoons. (father of 14-year-old daughter)

We joined a gym, a sort of health club place. I work out over my lunch hour, but on Saturday mornings I take the kids and they fool around and we play racquetball. (father of 13-year-old son)

Often the activities are linked to a chore or some other time commitment that is expanded to include some fun time:

I do the grocery shopping on Wednesday nights and Andy goes along. Ellen works at the store that night, so she doesn't get home till late, so we'll usually stop off and play a game of pool and shoot the breeze with some guys from work. (father of 14-year-old son)

I have ballet class on Tuesdays, so dad picks me up after it and we go get a pizza. It's real nice, it's just the two of us, and I can tell him about school and stuff. (F, 15)

While some of this activity is specifically intended to give fathers and children time together, much of it is built around a specific family chore or is intended to relieve the mother for a while. This is especially noteworthy because most of the parents report very little family time and very few family activities, since the teens have their own interests and activities, or "don't want to be seen in public with their parents" (mother of 16-year-old daughter).

Significantly, fathers are seldom confidants for their children. Only one father in the sample plays a highly nurturing role:

I've always tried to put them first. My dad was always busy and distant, and I always said I wasn't going to be like that. . . . Yeah, I changed diapers, and stayed up with sick kids, and have just always tried to be there for them. (father of 16-year-old daughter)

Two teens in married families and one teen in a divorced family feel they are able to confide in their fathers, at least about some things. Overall, however, most do not:

No, I don't tell him much about my problems or stuff. . . . I don't know, he's not home a lot. I guess that's it. (M, 15)

It's kind of hard to talk to him. I think it sort of makes him uncomfortable. (F, 17)

Various reasons are given for not confiding in fathers, including accessibility:

He's gone a lot at night, at work or meetings. You can't talk to somebody that's not home. (F, 15)

Most of the time, if we're both home, he sleeps. You know, we have dinner, and he turns on the TV and falls asleep. (M, 16)

Others say that their fathers are not the sort of person that you just sit and talk to, while others suggest it is just easier to talk to their mothers.

This is one area in which fathers are uncomfortable and, at times, defensive:

> I think they could talk to me if they wanted to. You know teenagers—they don't talk to their parents about anything. (father of 14-year-old son)

> Well, sure, we talk . . . it depends on what you mean. I think I have a pretty good idea of what's going on with them. If you're talking about sitting around spilling your guts and agonizing over stuff, well, kids don't talk to their parents about that. Did you talk to your parents about that stuff? Kids talk about those things to each other. (father of a 16-year-old son)

Others willingly admit, sometimes regretfully, that they do not talk to their children and are not confided in by them:

> No, we don't talk much. I'm not sure why. . . . Their mother did a lot of that, and I was working. I wish we did talk, but at this point it seems too late—I can't exactly say to him, "Well, son, tell me what you've been thinking for the past 15 years." (father of 15-year-old son)

> I guess it's my fault. I'm not very comfortable, you know, opening up to people. We've been married 20 years, and even my wife says I'm not an easy person to talk to. (father of 14-year-old son)

While some fathers draw on the stereotype of uncommunicative teenagers to explain their relationship, others take responsibility for the situation. For some, it is just the kind of person they are, or the way they have been brought up. For others, it is a pattern established early in their children's lives, when they were at work and their wives were responsible for child rearing. For most it is a situation that they are not altogether happy with.

FATHERS AND MOTHERS

Clearly, fathers and mothers play different roles in the support networks of their adolescent children. While overall the mother-adolescent relationship is closer than the father-adolescent relationship, fathers are more likely than mothers to spend time with their teens specifically engaging in fun activities. Most of the time mothers spend with their children consists of dealing with their everyday needs and problems, or of being with them while taking care of other responsibilities, such as preparing a meal.

The lower involvement of fathers in the daily lives of their children may help to explain why there is less overt conflict between fathers and teens than between mothers and teens. Much of the conflict that occurs in these families concerns relatively minor, common problems, such as needing or wanting something, whether it be clothes, money, or use of the car, or such things as talking on the telephone or doing homework, matters that are almost always handled by mothers. Furthermore, even though fathers commonly serve as authority figures, mothers are the enforcers. Mothers have the responsibility of relaying, explaining, and often justifying rules and decisions to their children, who are not always happy with the outcomes. Thus, mothers hear much of the complaining and have to deal with the resistance. Also, disciplining children for rule infractions is almost always the mother's chore, with the father serving in a backup capacity, and almost always more symbolically than in actions.

Even though fathers spend less time with their children than do mothers, the time spent with them tends to be more enjoyable for both parties, focusing on "fun activities" or outings. This may be a continuation of early patterns in the division of labor between mothers and fathers. It appears that fathers devote more of their time to play than do mothers when their children are infants (Kotelchuck, 1976; Lamb, 1977; Richards et al., 1977). Although not asked specifically about early experiences, a few fathers touch on this theme spontaneously:

> I've always liked doing things with the kids, taking them off somewhere, or fooling around. Unfortunately, I haven't always had the time. (father of 13-year-old son)

Other fathers speak of rediscovering or, in some cases, discovering their children as they get older:

> I feel like I know a little better what to do with them. I have to admit I never much liked reading to them or sitting forever and playing some game over and over again. Now, I can do stuff I like or know how to do, and I can do it with them. (father of 16-year-old son)

> I think I was always close to all three of them [daughters], but as they got older, it was different. They're really adults with ideas and things they want to share. They're three of my favorite people to just sit and talk with. (father of 16-year-old daughter)

The father-adolescent relationship may be related to patterns of marital satisfaction over the life cycle. Despite some methodological flaws, most research finds evidence of a U-shaped curve of satisfaction that hits its lowest point when there are teenagers in the home and starts upward again when the children have left (Rollins and Cannon, 1974; Rollins and Feldman, 1970; Spanier et al., 1975). Significantly, the decrease in satisfaction during the children's teenage years is not as significant for husbands as it is for wives (Spanier and Lewis, 1980). If, in fact, there is a tendency for mothers to get bogged down in the routine and sometimes frustrating tasks of child care, while fathers are able to concentrate more of their time with children in leisure activities, there could very well be negative effects on marital satisfaction.

This is not to imply that the father-teen relationship is all good while the mother-teen relationship is all bad. In fact, considering the likelihood of being listed as a support, the likelihood of being seen as a confidante, and the teens' self-reports of their closeness to each parent, clearly the mother-adolescent relationship, on average, is closer than the father-adolescent relationship. While teenagers recognize and appreciate the shared time with their fathers, when they define support they suggest that other things are equally, and probably more, important. The role of the mother as a confidante and the fact that she is the one who deals directly with their everyday, ongoing needs and concerns, means that despite the increased conflict that can result, teenagers see their mothers as more supportive and their relationships as being closer.

FATHERS AFTER DIVORCE

Twenty of the teenagers are not residing with their biological fathers due to the divorce of their parents. Ten are living with their divorced mother and ten are living with their divorced mother and stepfather. It is possible to consider the impact of divorce on the father-adolescent relationship by looking at the frequency and amount of contact between noncustodial fathers and their teenage children, and the substantive aspects of the noncustodial father role. Since no noncustodial fathers were interviewed, conclusions are limited to adolescents' and mothers' perceptions of the divorced fathers' roles.

The frequency and amount of contact between divorced fathers and their adolescents vary considerably, but overall are not very high. The typical arrangement is on the order of a daylong visit or perhaps a weekend every three to four weeks. Four of the adolescents whose parents are divorced have had no contact with their father in the previous three years, and two of those four have not seen their father at all since the divorce. One adolescent sees her father weekly, and several others visit every other week. When the parents reside some distance apart, it is not unusual to have the children spend the summer and holidays with the father. Most of the teens have occasional contact between visits through phone calls, letters and cards, and gifts.

By most accounts the contact has decreased in frequency over time. In part, fathers maintain temporarily high levels of contact immediately following separation, in an attempt to stay connected and, perhaps, to ease feelings of loneliness and disruption. However, as those involved settle into a routine, perhaps move to a new locale, and establish new contacts and ties, visitation becomes less frequent, a finding supported by others (Furstenberg and Spanier, 1984; Hetherington et al., 1978). Furthermore, the children are older than at the time of the divorce. Others have noted that contact is negatively related to the age of the child (Wallerstein and Kelly, 1979), and that frequent contact is more difficult with teenagers as they develop their own interests and peer interaction becomes more important (Weiss, 1975). This is a theme echoed in the teens' responses:

> I used to spend the summers with him and the Christmas break, up until this summer. I used to like going there because it was a chance to get away and he'd buy us things and take us to the beach and stuff. . . . [This summer] I didn't want to leave because my friends were here and we had made plans to do stuff together, like have parties and hang out at the pool. . . . He didn't seem to mind that much. I mean, he's busy at work and stuff. (F, 15)

> I don't know, really [why contact has decreased]. I guess we kind of ran out of things to do or something like that. You know, we used to go places or something, but I don't much want to do that stuff anymore. (M, 17)

The mothers, too, note that contact has decreased, and link it to the decreasing child support they receive over time:

> Just overall he's not taking as much responsibility—he doesn't take them as often, he buys them fewer things, and, of course, the checks are getting smaller and smaller. (mother of 15-year-old daughter)

All but three of the divorced mothers received child support at the time of the divorce, but not one is currently receiving as much as they had originally, even though the children's needs and expenses have increased.

The small sample size and the lack of interviews with noncustodial fathers make it difficult to determine exactly what factors contribute to decreasing contact. While some researchers find that contact is not affected by the gender of the child (Furstenberg et al., 1983), others find that boys have more contact with their fathers after divorce than do girls (Hess and Camara, 1979). Furstenberg and colleagues (1983) find that education has a positive effect on contact, black fathers have less contact than white fathers, and contact is higher when the parents, especially mothers, remain single. Furthermore, they find no evidence of greater contact among more recent cohorts of divorced fathers, and while proximity may make contact easier, it is no guarantee. Some research also suggests that the amount of interparental support and conflict is not a significant predictor of the amount of father-child contact (Bowman and Ahrons, 1985).

Among the teens, there is little evidence that gender affects the likelihood or amount of contact with the father. Only in the extreme cases of no contact between father and child does the mother-father relationship appear to affect the father-child relationship:

> He had been abusive to both of us—blaming us for the problems he had been having. There was absolutely no desire on the part of any of us for him to continue seeing either one of us. (mother of 16-year-old son)

> In the four years we were married he had been totally irresponsible— he was immature and certainly not ready to be a father. When I moved with the kids, he never made any effort to see them or find out about them. (mother of 17-year-old son)

In the remaining cases there is a good deal of variation in the mother-father relationship after divorce. However, most of the mothers recognize the importance of continued interaction with the father and are making an effort not to let their feelings influence the children.

The teenagers, however, are not always immune to the feelings of their parents:

> It's hard sometimes, knowing that the two of them are still really angry with each other. When I come back from seeing him, I always feel kind of like I have to be sort of careful, like, you know, so she won't think I liked being there better than with her. (F, 14)

Furthermore, a few of the teens admit that they have at one time or another used visitation to express their own hurt and anger:

> At first I didn't go to see him at all. I thought he could have done something to make her [mother] stay. (M, 17)

> Yeah, I was really mad at both of them. My dad would call and I wouldn't talk to him, or he'd come to get me and I wouldn't be here. Then, it was kind of weird, I thought maybe my mom kind of was happy about it, like I liked her best or something, so I started going to see him a lot. It was crazy. Now I do what I want to do. (F, 15)

This response is most common in the first year or two after divorce, until feelings of anger and hurt subside somewhat.

While proximity makes contact easier, it is no guarantee. Those teens who live closest to their fathers (about half reside in the same town) do not necessarily see their fathers most frequently. Ironically, proximity can have the opposite effect by making contact less routinized and more haphazard:

> Yeah, I could see him more often, but it's like I got things to do and so does he, and, well, it's not that big a deal, so if I don't see him this week, it's not like I have to wait months or anything. I mean, he lives right here. (M, 15)

On the other hand, when father and child are separated by some distance, a more concerted effort has to be made for contact to occur, and routinization of contact thus becomes very important. As one mother puts it:

> When he moved west, we were both pretty sensitive to the fact that it would be very easy for Sharon to lose touch with him, and neither one of us wanted that. So we were very careful to plan out exactly when he would see her—which holidays and for how long, and when he would call her in between. He's been out there seven years, and I can't think of a single time when we changed the plan. (mother of 16-year-old daughter)

Thus, the more routinized the contact, the more frequent it is and the more likely it is to continue, regardless of the physical distance between father and child.

With respect to satisfaction with the amount of contact, the most common attitude is one of resigned acceptance:

> Sure, I guess I'd like to see him more. But I know he and my mom can't live together, so what're you going to do? (M, 14)

Perhaps because of their ages and their changing interests, children recognize that the amount of contact they have is not solely their fathers' responsibility. As one teen uneasily puts it:

> I guess, sure, it would be nice to see him more. But then, I could if I really wanted to. You know, he doesn't live far away, and I could call him up or something. But . . . I don't know, I have stuff to do and it's just, like, the time just goes by. (F, 14)

This may be one reason why very few of the adolescents express hurt or anger concerning the limited degree of contact. Most have a realistic view of the situation and, in fact, accept some of the responsibility for what transpires between their fathers and themselves.

As for fathers' roles in the teenagers' support networks, there are differences as well as similarities between custodial and noncustodial fathers. While custodial fathers are almost always important authority figures for their children, at least symbolically, it is difficult for noncustodial fathers to play this role:

> He doesn't make my rules anymore. I mean, if I'm at his house, there's stuff I don't do, but it's not the same. It's not every day, or like he expects me to do it all the time. (F, 13)

This partly is due to his absence from the home and the fact that mothers rarely invoke a noncustodial father as a final authority. Few, in fact, consult him about problems with, or decisions concerning, the children:

> No, I don't talk to him about my decisions. Why should I? I'm the one that has to live with them. (mother of 14-year-old daughter)

A few mothers consult their ex-husbands about disciplinary problems or decisions, almost always when the mother feels that her authority is being undermined:

> He would let them run wild. They'd come back on Sunday and they

were just impossible. You know, it was "Dad didn't make us . . . ,"
or "Dad let us . . ," or "Why do we have to . . . ?" I'd spend three
days justifying to them all over again why we had certain rules. I
finally called and said it had to stop. (mother of 14-year-old daughter)

While the majority of the teens in divorced families have continued contact
with their fathers and spend significant amounts of time in his home, they
see his authority as extending only to the time that they are in his care:

Sure, he's got rules and things I gotta do when I'm there, but it's not
a big thing, and it's just when I'm there. (M, 14)

Well, like it's pretty much the same with him and my mom. You
know, most of the stuff we do at home is OK with him. He might let
us stay up later, or like one time, we ate ice cream sundaes for supper,
but it's always a treat or something. He'll say, "Now don't go pulling
this on your mom, this is just for tonight." (F, 14)

Thus, when the parents are divorced, there is a subtle shift in the family's
authority relations. The mother is the initiator and the final authority in
most decisions, rather than being the one who carries out decisions made
by the father.

The father's declining authority also is related to his declining importance as an economic provider. In all 20 previously or currently divorced
families, the majority of the family's income is either the mother's or the
stepfather's earnings, or both. Child support is minimal, and decreases and
becomes less regular over time.

One way in which noncustodial fathers can make up for their decreased
significance as authority figure or provider, and prevent declining attachment on the part of their children, is to provide them with gifts, shopping
trips, and other tangible signs of their continued concern and involvement
(Furstenberg and Spanier, 1984; Weiss, 1975). Whether or not this is the
father's motivation, this kind of interaction is very common:

I used to like going there [to father's house] because it was a chance
to get away, and he'd buy us things and take us to the beach and stuff.
(F, 15)

They [mother and father] have it worked out where he always buys
our shoes and winter coats and stuff. But he's all the time giving us
stuff—something we say we need or something he knows I'd really
like but mom can't get it. (M, 14)

It is not a situation that altogether pleases the mothers, often interpreted as an attempt by the father to "buy the children's affection" or to get back at her:

> Every time she goes there, we practically have to send an empty suitcase with her to bring back all the stuff he gets her. Last summer she was crazy about skateboards and she forgot hers when she left. So I called him up to say I'd send it and he said no big deal, he'd already been out to get her a new one, and of course it was twice as expensive as the one I had gotten. I tell him not to, that he doesn't have to buy her things, she'll still love him, and he just says he wants to do it, he likes giving her things. And I think, well, maybe it's me, maybe I'm just jealous because I can't buy her the things I'd like to. (mother of 16-year-old daughter)

At times the situation is exacerbated by minimal child support:

> It really kills me. He's more than willing to buy them all the stuff they don't need so they can think what a great guy he is, but I have to scrape just to get them the things they need. Karen had all this dental work done—I've got over $300 of dentist bills in the drawer and don't know how I'm going to pay them. But I ask him for help and he reminds me that we agreed I'd take care of medical expenses because of my insurance. But this isn't even covered. And she'll come home next weekend with $50 worth of new clothes and things that she could have lived without. (mother of 14-year-old daughter)

Whether the father-child relationship is affected by or dependent upon his gift buying is debatable. Clearly it is an aspect of the noncustodial father role that the teens take for granted.

Besides gift-giving, the "weekend father" phenomenon involves entertaining the children with outings and excursions, and letting them do things they do not ordinarily do (Furstenberg and Spanier, 1984; Leupnitz, 1982). About two-thirds of the teens (14) describe visits with their fathers as typically spent doing something fun or going somewhere on an outing, which is particularly striking since only 16 of the teens have any regular contact with their fathers. Common activities include shopping trips, eating at restaurants, seeing movies, attending sporting events, and, especially with younger teens, going to a zoo or amusement park. As the adolescents get older, they lose interest in these sorts of activities. Finding a suitable alternative is not easy; indeed, in many cases contact drops in frequency as the children get too old for outings. Some continue to visit their fathers but actually spend little time interacting with them, using the visits to get back to the old neighborhood or to spend time with nearby friends.

Sometimes fathers and children participate in joint activities or projects, such as working on a car or helping the father furnish and decorate a new apartment. At times it is difficult for the adolescents to describe how their time is spent during visitation:

Just ordinary stuff, I guess. Like, well, we watch TV, we watch football. Just hang out, I guess. You know, I'm there. (M, 15)

Yeah, we talk some. I mean, I tell him about school or stuff. We maybe go out for lunch, or send out for pizza. I don't know what we do, really. I know that sounds pretty dumb, but the time just kind of goes by. (F, 14)

Even among the older adolescents and those with infrequent contact with their fathers, birthdays in particular evoke the "weekend father." On birthdays the adolescents can count on some extra display of affection, including expensive gifts, dinner out, or other special treatment. Possibly birthdays take on a special significance because they are tangible symbols of the biological tie between fathers and children. Furstenberg and Spanier (1984) argue that fathers may stress the biological dimension of the father-child tie as their capacity to fulfill their social obligations as authorities and providers is diminished. The lack of fathers' perspectives precludes drawing conclusions about their motivations and interpretations. While fathers may use birthdays to reassert biological ties, an alternative explanation is possible. In American society the gift-giving, parties, and special treatment of birthdays are ritualized. For divorced fathers they may be particularly convenient as well as expected times around when to center interaction. Teenagers in divorced families describe similar interaction and responses at Christmas as well as other holidays.

Considerable support is obtained for divorced fathers as the stereotypical "weekend fathers." However, strikingly similar patterns of interaction are identified among adolescents and custodial fathers, particularly with respect to excursions and fun activities. Many custodial fathers are able to make routine household activities into leisure activities shared with the children. Thus, much of the shared time arises out of the everyday fact of being in the same household and having to see that certain things get done. The "weekend father" role may in fact be an especially convenient role for fathers to play regardless of whether they share a residence with their children. However, while the frequency of gift-giving and fun leisure activities does not distinguish between custodial and noncustodial fathers, the contexts of their interaction do. For divorced fathers, this tends to be the primary, if not the only, role they play, whereas married fathers have more options, including authority figure, role model, and economic provider.

When divorced fathers are compared with divorced mothers, a striking difference emerges in the area of parent-child confiding. About half of the teens talk to their noncustodial fathers about matters of interest to them, but are less likely to talk to them about problems or more personal matters. This is especially clear when they compare their relationships with their fathers and their relationships with their mothers:

> Oh, they're pretty different. I don't talk to my dad like I talk to my mom, you know, about problems and things that are really important to me. I don't know why, really. Well, I guess because he doesn't live here and he doesn't know about a lot of the things I do and the people I know and stuff. But even then, if he did, I'm not sure I'd talk to him like I do my mom. He's a different kind of person. He doesn't really open up a lot, and he's real busy with work and stuff, so we never really do sit around and just talk about stuff. (F, 16)

> I don't see him all that much, so when I do go, we like to talk and catch up on things . . but it's more like how I'm doing in school, and if I'm playing basketball, or stuff that's going on with people I know. (M, 14)

The adolescents frequently suggest that since their fathers are not around, it is especially difficult to fill them in on personal matters. Furthermore, several doubt that they would do so even if they shared a residence, citing the father's personality or the relatively greater ease with which they can talk to and confide in their mothers.

The most significant difference between divorced mothers and fathers is that none of the teens feel that their fathers confide in them. Certainly this is due in part to the convenience of sharing a residence and the ready availability of mothers for providing personal support. Divorced fathers, on the other hand, see their children only intermittently, making personal interaction more problematic. Most of the teens, however, explain it as some facet of the father's personality:

He's not much of a talker. I don't think he even talked to my mom all that much when they were married. (F, 15)

I guess he's kind of a quiet person, like shy or something. I guess I'm kind of like that, too. (M, 13)

Since custodial divorced fathers are not included, it is impossible to determine to what extent structural factors are responsible. In other words, it is possible that residential divorced father-adolescent relationships would not differ significantly from residential divorced mother-adolescent relationships. However, caution is necessary for two reasons. First, while confiding between parents and children in married households is less frequent, it is more common between mothers and adolescents. Second, men who are currently fathers of adolescents are likely to be affected by gender socialization, making men less likely to open up and feel comfortable discussing personal matters. In her study of custody arrangements Leupnitz (1982) found that one-fourth of the fathers in her sample stated that there was no one, either pre- or post-divorce, in whom they confided.

REMARRIAGE, FATHERS, AND STEPFATHERS

Ten of the adolescents are currently living with a stepfather. The average length of remarriage is close to four years, ranging from one and a half to nine years. Five of the stepfathers have been previously married, and three have children from an earlier marriage. In one such case the stepfather is a widower with three children, and his wife is divorced with custody of her three children. Their remarriage resulted in a reconstituted family including six children, all teenagers at the time of the remarriage. Another remarried family consists of a divorced mother, her son, a stepfather, and two daughters born after the remarriage. In the remaining eight cases the only children residing in the home are the children from the wife's previous marriage.

Regardless of how long they have been remarried, everyone agrees that remarriage requires definite adjustments by all concerned, and never without at least minor difficulties:

Oh, yeah, it took some getting used to. You know, just getting used to having another person around. In a way I guess it's like having a house guest, you're not quite comfortable or just can't, like, be yourself. But this house guest isn't going home in a week. He's here for good. (mother of 15-year-old son)

It took me some time to get used to it. Just weird things used to bug me ... well, like, we had always had supper at 6:00, but Jay [stepfather] never got home from work till then, so we had supper later and I used to complain about it all the time. (M, 13)

Others have more serious difficulties:

For two years not a day went by when I didn't ask myself whether we'd made a big mistake. It was two years of constant battling—me and Chuck, Chuck and the kids, me and the kids. Nobody was happy. (mother of 14-year-old daughter)

They readily identify things they would do differently, given another chance:

I think the biggest mistake we made was for the four of us to move into his house. His kids had already established it as sort of their territory, and we were the intruders. (mother of 17-year-old daughter)

I guess I moved too fast. I wanted to really be their father, but I didn't give them much of a chance to even get to know me. Yeah, I would take it slower, things like that take time. (stepfather of 15-year-old daughter)

Adjustment is hardest during the first few years following remarriage, but for the most part has improved over time. All but two of the remarried families characterize adjustment as a continuous, ongoing process.

Three areas of family life are particularly problematic for remarried families, at times causing considerable conflict and always requiring some readjustment. First, there are problems revolving around the addition of a new member to the divorced mother-children subsystem, including establishing a new routine and household rules, and getting used to another person with different personality traits, habits, and experiences. Anytime a new member is added to a group, some adjustment in patterns of interacting and relationships will be required. The addition of a stepfather to a mother-child group is no exception. When the respondents are asked to describe the adjustments that have to be made, their lists are long:

It made me mad that the kids still just kept going to their mom for stuff and just ignored my even being there. (stepfather of 13-year-old daughter)

I had gotten used to making my own decisions, and it was tough having to include another person in that, and sometimes having to give in. (mother of 16-year-old daughter)

Bedtimes, mealtimes, television, talking on the phone, using the car, curfews—you name it, we had to work it out all over again. (mother of 17-year-old daughter)

He never liked what I wanted to see on TV. Now I have my own. (M, 13)

The problems often are not serious or unusual, but they are exacerbated by at least two factors. First, most married couples have time to establish their couple relationship before having to deal with children (Furstenberg and Spanier, 1984). Second, the divorced mother-adolescent subsystem is a particularly close one. Indeed, many seemingly trivial arguments in remarried families actually may concern whether the mother-child subsystem will continue to be the dominant one (Papernow, 1984).

Over time, there is less "side taking" and more cooperative negotiation:

It had gotten to be a big problem. Before we were married, Ed and I had never discussed the kids' rules and things, and I guess a lot of it was my fault because I assumed we'd just stick with my rules. I didn't think he might have ideas of his own about how things ought to be done. So we were arguing about everything, and the kids were picking up on it and really using it till finally we sat down and made lists of everything, all the rules and stuff we thought were important, and we settled on it all. Sometimes I gave in, sometimes he did. Then we took it to the kids and said this is it, this is the way it is. (mother of 14-year-old son)

I guess my mom was pretty smart. I'd complain about him [step-father] or something he did, and she'd make me go to him, you know, like she'd say, "This is your problem, so you have to work it out together," and sometimes she'd tell him there was something on my mind, and then we'd talk it out. (F, 16)

Some of the problems, however, are more difficult and more painful to deal with because they threaten the particularly close mother-adolescent relationship that develops after divorce, involving mutual confiding and emotional support. Most of the mothers feel that the marital relationship should take precedence and that it is inappropriate to confide in the teen when the husband is available, particularly about matters concerning him.

The consequent changes in the mother-child relationship are recognized by both adolescents and mothers, although the mothers find it somewhat easier to accept:

> It had to change. It just wouldn't have worked out any other way. And I know it was hard on Jenny [daughter], but I would like to think that we're still closer than we were before I divorced, and looking at a lot of the people I know, I'm sure we're a lot closer than most other mothers and daughters. You know, we learned to trust each other and depend on each other to get through. So I think we're still really close even if we don't spend as much time together or there are things we don't talk about. (mother of 16-year-old daughter)

Resentment on the part of the adolescents is common despite concerted efforts by the families to resolve the problem.

A second set of problems revolves around balancing the rights, obligations, and responsibilities of the biological noncustodial father and the stepfather. Furstenberg and Spanier (1984) find that a certain amount of rivalry and jealousy is almost inevitable, and although remarriage often results in decreased contact between nonresidential fathers and their children, it is not clear whether this is a cause or an effect of rivalry. In the eight cases where there is contact with the noncustodial father following the mother's remarriage, all of the families have some difficulties in this area:

> Yeah, I was jealous. Here I was the one living with them and doing the best I could, supporting them and trying to make it easier on them, but it was like I was a total stranger. They'd go off to spend the weekend, and when they got back, it was all they talked about. [stepfather of 13-year-old son)

> I think Jack [ex-husband] was really jealous, like he had to compete. Before Ted [stepfather] and I got married, it was no problem with the kids, he agreed to pretty much follow my rules. But after, it was just a whole different story. (mother of 14-year-old daughter)

> I think that what really bugged me most of all was that the guy [noncustodial father] was a real jerk. He had never paid any attention to them before the divorce, and he just about had to be forced to see them afterward, and he never did any more than he had to. And here I was, you know, I really loved those kids, I didn't have any of my own, and they were the only ones I was ever going to have, and it

seemed like no matter what I did, they'd push me away and go running back to him. (stepfather of 15-year-old daughter)

While these feelings tend to subside with time (Furstenberg and Spanier, 1984), it is not uncommon for jealousy or rivalry to resurface, even years after the remarriage:

We seem to have it worked out OK. Yeah, it's a problem sometimes when they get back from being with him [noncustodial father] for a while. They come home Sunday night and they talk about what they did and stuff. Sometimes I get tired of hearing about how much fun they had or what a great guy he is. (stepfather of 13-year-old daughter)

Indeed, "reentry" of the children into the remarried household after visitation is generally problematic. It is particularly acute for stepfathers, who feel, more than at any other time, that they are being compared with the father.

Usually the adolescents work out mutually acceptable relationships with both the stepfather and the biological father. At times this is an "either-or" situation in which a close relationship is established with one to the exclusion of the other. One adolescent has clearly drawn closer to the biological father since the remarriage:

He's my dad, and nothing will change that. If mom wasn't happy and had to marry Bob, well, that's the way it is, and it just means dad needs me even more. (M, 14)

In three cases, however, the relationship with the stepfather is especially close, with a concomitant decrease in contact and closeness with the biological father:

It's not so great going to see him anymore. I used to want to go 'cause I missed him and stuff, but, like, well, it's like I just would rather be here. Jim [stepfather] is a lot more like a dad, you know, like doing stuff with me. (M, 15)

Well, it was just really clear that my dad had a lot of problems. Like, I always thought he really cared and I should go see him because he was my dad, but then, with looking at the way John [stepfather] has been with us, and the stuff he's done, it's like I know now what being a dad is all about. You know, he's adopting us this year and that's really like it should be, 'cause he's really our dad in all the ways that count. (F, 16)

In these cases the stepfather serves as a contrast to the father, highlighting his short-comings and perhaps making it easier for unpleasant contact to be discontinued.

In many other cases a suitable arrangement is worked out by drawing clear distinctions between the relationship with the father and that with the stepfather:

They're pretty different. I don't know, Tom [stepfather] is more like a father, I guess, because I've lived with him four years now and I'm the youngest, so he made a lot of the decisions with my mom when I was starting to go out and things like that. My dad, I guess, as I've gotten older, he's more sort of a friend, but I don't really see him as a father. (F, 17)

I do stuff with my dad that I don't do with Jack [stepfather], and Jack's, like, showed me other stuff, like hunting. (M, 13)

As long as there is some division or distinction in the relationship, and it is not felt that one is trying to impinge on the other's territory, teenagers seem capable of maintaining mutually satisfactory relationships with both the father and the stepfather.

Often symptomatic of struggles between fathers and stepfathers is the issue of names and kinship designations, which has been noted as a particularly sensitive issue in many remarried families (Cherlin, 1978; Furstenberg and Spanier, 1984). Three adolescents refer to their step-fathers as "dad." In one such case there has been no contact with the father since the divorce, in one there has been no contact in three years, and in the other contact is scattered and minimal. In two of these cases legal adoption proceedings have been started or carried out, with a concomitant adoption of the stepfather's surname. In two remarried families the target adolescent calls the stepfather by his first name and at least one younger sibling calls him "dad." In general, using kinship designations for step-parents is more likely when the child is young and when there is little or no contact with the biological parent (Furstenberg and Spanier, 1984). Despite continuing awkwardness about names, all have reached some mutually acceptable agreement. Just as the teens find it necessary to distinguish clearly between their relationships with the father and the stepfather, so they find it necessary to distinguish between them in their names. In only one case, where contact with the biological father is infrequent and brief, does the adolescent use "dad" to refer to both the father and the stepfather.

A third and related category of problems concerns negotiating a suitable role for the stepfather to play with respect to the children. Residential biological fathers are likely to serve as authority figures, role models, and companions who enjoy joint leisure activities with the children. Nonresidential biological fathers are less likely to act as authority figures and role models, but are very likely to play the "weekend father" role. All of these roles are difficult for stepfathers to adopt and carry out successfully:

> It was a real problem all right. I guess they really resented me for awhile. They didn't want to do anything I said. You know, I still can't say that I'm a real authority, or anything like that, but I think I have a little more say as to what goes on. (stepfather of 14-year-old son)

> You have to remember we had six teenagers in the house, and I think being an authority is always a problem with them anyway. You know, they think they're adults and they find one way after another to test that. So we really had to find a different way to approach it so it didn't seem like I was forcing my rules on them. We did a lot of family meeting type of things, and a lot of negotiating. It was pretty complex sometimes. (stepfather of 17-year-old daughter)

The adolescents concur:

> Well, it's not like I need a lot of rules or anything. Most of that was worked out with my mom. I guess if something really bugged him, he'd tell my mom. But if you mean telling me what to do and stuff, no, he doesn't do that. (F, 16)

> I don't like it when he tells me what to do. It just doesn't seem right. You know, like my mom can do that. (M, 13)

Stepfathers are more likely to act and to be accepted as authority figures when the children are relatively young at the time of the remarriage. Otherwise, the stepfather is unlikely to see himself or to be seen by the stepchildren as an authority figure.

The children's resentment and unwillingness to recognize him as a legitimate member of the household are partially responsible. However, these teens, particularly the older ones, are beginning to assert their own independence and authority, generally seeing their parents less as rule makers and enforcers and more as joint negotiators. Indeed, what many parents see as most troublesome about dealing with adolescents is the constant debating and negotiating. Of course, married fathers have an advantage, having established themselves as authority figures earlier in their children's lives. Thus, many of their rules and values have already been internalized. Stepfathers, on the other hand, have spent significantly less time with the children.

For some of the same reasons it is difficult for stepfathers to be "weekend fathers." Some have tried this approach as a way of winning over the children in the beginning of the marriage, but find it further undermines their attempts to exert authority and control over the children. Nonetheless, stepfathers are significant sources of support in the adolescents' networks. Five of the teens listed their stepfathers in their initial descriptions of their support networks, and several others note later in the interview that they provide some sort of support.

While it is relatively easy to describe the roles stepfathers do not play, it is more difficult to accurately portray what roles they do play. What stands out is the diversity and variability in the relationships with stepfathers:

> He's the only person I ever fight with. And I mean we fight about everything, and all the time. My mom says it's the only way we know . . . to say anything to each other because it's all we ever do. . . . I would really miss him a lot if he wasn't there. I mean, we don't talk about problems and he doesn't seem like a father, and I guess it sounds kind of funny because I said he gives me support. I don't think I can explain it. I can't really tell you what he does for me, but I know I would really miss him if he left, and it's not just because I'm used to him being there. We really are close to each other, and our fighting all the time is just how we talk to each other, or how we get close to each other. (F, 16)

> Well, like, he's just the way he is. He's here and he'll tell me about stuff. Sometimes I go to work with him and help out if I'm not in school. (M, 14)

> He does a lot of stuff for me. He takes me to baseball and, like, he went to every one of my football games that he could get off for. I guess dads do that, but it's different. He was at more games than anybody else's dad and, like, it's because he really likes it. He doesn't push me or anything. There's another guy—his dad goes but it's like

he just stands there and hollers about what he's doing wrong. It's not like that at all. (M, 15)

In fact, those stepfathers who have worked out close, enjoyable, and mutually acceptable relationships with their stepchildren are those who are not bound by a particular role, but interact with the stepchild as an individual. Stepchildren are more likely than biological children to describe the stepfather's personality, or his interests and characteristics, in explaining the role he plays in the support network. The viability of this approach for stepparent-stepchild relations is supported by recent research. While earlier research assumes that the parental role is the best role for the stepparent, and focuses on the problems encountered in trying to play that role, more recent research suggests that the parental role is not necessarily the only or the best option open to stepfathers, especially with adolescents (Mills, 1984). Other options include uncle, teacher, coach, companion, and possibly many others. Furthermore, the role that the stepparent plays in the family is often based on special qualities or idiosyncrasies that may, in fact, have led to earlier conflicts (Papernow, 1984).

Previous research has suggested that adjustment to a stepparent is affected by the child's age (Bernard, 1956; Robinson, 1984; Wallerstein and Kelly, 1980) and sex (Clingempeel et al., 1984; Santrock et al., 1982; Wallerstein and Kelly, 1980). The retrospective accounts of the adolescents and parents interviewed clearly suggest that younger children make an easier and faster adjustment to a stepfather than do older children. Evidence of a gender difference, however, is not strong. It is possible that any gender differences that occur are most acute in the beginning of the remarriage. Several stepfathers report that it has taken them longer to work out enjoyable and comfortable relationships with their stepdaughters because they feel less comfortable with girls than with boys. This is not surprising, given the persistence of gender-based socialization and the emphasis on gender-appropriate interests and activities.

CONCLUSIONS

Fathers are important members of adolescent support networks, although they quantitatively and qualitatively differ from mothers. Overall, fathers are seldom confidants or everyday problem solvers, but they are more likely than mothers to spend time with their teens in fun, leisure activities, acting as "weekend fathers" regardless of their marital status.

Concomitantly, there is less overt conflict in the father-adolescent relationship than in the mother-adolescent relationship.

Fathers in married families see themselves, and are seen by their children, as authority figures. Divorced fathers find this more difficult due to decreased contact and an attenuated role as family provider. Thus, they concentrate even more time and energy in the "weekend father" role. Stepfathers also face difficulties in working out a suitable role. Limited joint histories and shared residences make it problematic for stepfathers to be authority figures or weekend fathers. The result is more diversity and variability in stepfather-stepchild relationships, based on the individual traits and interests of the stepfather.

Fathers and mothers both play another, more indirect role in the support networks of their children. From very early ages they provide them with a set of kin from whom they can draw support. To what extent this support is significant, and the degree to which it is affected by living arrangements, is yet to be seen.

6

Adolescents and Their Relatives

Besides being important sources of support in their own right, parents are key members of adolescent networks because of their links with other potentially supportive individuals, especially other adults. Through their parents children are incorporated into a network of kin—grandparents, aunts, uncles, cousins, and so on. Parents can also connect their children to numerous other adults by calling on them to baby-sit or chauffeur, or by bringing the children into contact with ministers, doctors, or counselors, or by drawing family friends into the family network.

In the case of young children it is safe to assert that the family's network is the child's network. Aside from age-peers, most young children are dependent upon their parents to initiate and maintain ties with other people. A child is likely to have frequent contact with relatives if the parents have frequent contact with them; however, if the parents have little or no contact with relatives, it is highly unlikely that a young child will independently initiate such contact. It remains to be seen whether the same is true for adolescents, who may be in a better position to form and activate relations independently of their parents. At the very least they may discontinue contact with persons they do not particularly like but interact with because of their parents. The older they get and the broader their social worlds become, the more likely it will be that adolescents will build their own support networks.

Focusing on adolescents' relationships with adult relatives raises several questions for consideration. How frequently do adolescents include relatives in their support networks, and are some relatives more likely to be included than others? What types of support, if any, do relatives provide for adolescents? How does parents' marital status affect adolescents' contact with and feelings about their relatives? Does remarriage provide adolescents with another set of kin? To what extent are stepparents' relatives drawn into adolescents' support networks?

ADOLESCENTS AND GRANDPARENTS

Grandparents are by far the relatives most frequently included in the adolescents' support networks. This is somewhat surprising, since the teenagers are presumably beyond the appropriate ages for the more common grandparenting behaviors like baby-sitting and home-centered recreational activities, such as reading stories or playing games (Robertson, 1977). All but three of the adolescents have at least one living grandparent. The distribution of the adolescents by how many and which grandparents are living is shown in Table 4. Over half of the teens have at least three living grand-parents. More grandmothers than grandfathers are living, and slightly more maternal than paternal grandparents are living.

With few exceptions (Kivett, 1985), research suggests that the grand-parent role is seen as important by grandparents, is widely enjoyed, and

Table 4
Distribution of Adolescents by Number and Kin Position
of Living Grandparents

	Number of Teenagers	Percent
Number of Living Grandparents		
None	3	10.0
One	2	6.7
Two	8	26.7
Three	13	43.3
Four	4	13.3
Kin Position of Living Grandparents		
Maternal Grandmother	23	76.7
Maternal Grandfather	16	53.3
Paternal Grandmother	20	66.7
Paternal Grandfather	14	46.7

perhaps is important for mental health (Kivnick, 1982; Robertson, 1977). Increasingly it appears that grandparents are important to grandchildren and may in fact have some impact on their well-being (Baranowski, 1982; Barranti, 1985; Kornhaber and Woodward, 1981; Matthews and Sprey, 1985). Among the teens interviewed, deep emotional bonds with grandparents are common. Grandparents play significant supportive roles in the lives of their grandchildren even when they do not live within easy visiting distance:

> I really can't think of a single thing that my grandmother wouldn't do for me if I asked her to. (F, 14)

> My favorite people in the whole world are Nanna and PawPaw [paternal grandparents]. It seems like they always know when I need something. I don't even have to ask, they just know. (F, 17)

> Now my Grandpa Frank [maternal grandfather], he's a good one [support]. You know, not even my friends, no, you know, I can't think of anybody else that just has always taken me the way I am. It's funny, last year, when I had some trouble, my mom would say, "This'll kill your grandpa if he finds out." But he did find out, and he's the only one who really stood with me—my mom was the one with all the problems with it. (M, 17)

These sentiments are echoed time and time again. Emotional ties persist at times when illness or disability prevents grandparents from providing anything:

> My grandma, my mom's mom, is real important to me, but she doesn't really give me support or stuff like that because she's really sick and she's been in a nursing home for a long time. But I guess she's really important to me because I lived with her for two years after my parents divorced because my mom didn't have enough money to keep me with her. (F, 16)

Even teenagers whose grandparents are dead refer to them as previously important supports:

> The person I miss most is my Gramps. He died last year, but even when he was so sick, we talked on the phone every week. (M, 15)

> The worst thing that's happened to me, I think, is my Grandma dying. It was just like losing a really, really good friend. (F, 14)

You'll probably think this is weird, but, well, in some ways I'd have to say my Grandma gives me support even though she's dead. Lots of times I'll, like, think about things she'd told me, or how she'd handle stuff, things like that. (F, 15)

Two themes emerge from the grandparent-grandchild relationships that indicate the functions fulfilled by grandparents. The first is that of the grandparent as mediator between parents and child. In part this is reflected in the tendency of the teens to refer to their grandparents as "friends." Adolescents remark that they can talk to their grandparents about anything, or that the grandparent is a good listener. As such the grandparent can be considered a confidant, a finding supported by others (Baranowski, 1982; Updegraf, 1968). But, more specifically, grandparents are important in this capacity precisely because of their parental relationship with the adolescent's parents:

The funniest thing my Grandma'll do is when I'll be complaining about my mom or something, and my Grandma'll tell me how my mom was just like that when she was my age. So my mom, then, when she gets mad about something I did, I'll say, "Grandma said you always did the same thing when you were my age," and my mom will stop, and we'll start laughing, and then we get it all straight. (F, 15)

In this case the grandmother manages to defuse some of the conflict and tension between the parent and child. In fact, grandparents are frequently mentioned as persons the teens can talk to about problems with parents and who can be trusted not to tell the parents what has been said. Clearly the grandparents run some risk of being accused of taking sides and interfering in the parent-child relationship. Somehow, however, grandparents largely avoid fueling the parent-child conflict and manage to provide the teens with a new perspective on their parents. In this respect, grandparents are in a better position to deal with the teens' problems with parents than are age-peers. They not only listen to expressions of hurt and anger, but from their adult vantage point can help the teens work through the feelings and deal with them more constructively.

The second theme emerging from the grandparent-grandchild relationship concerns the grandparents' roles as creators and transmitters of a shared family history, a role identified as significant (Baranowski, 1982; Updegraf, 1968). Each grandchild has a set of past experiences, shared activities or skills, and anecdotes—a set of "family trivia"—that characterizes his or her relationships with grandparents. Sometimes hobbies or skills are learned from the grandparents, such as stamp collecting, gardening, or needlework. Others spontaneously mention anecdotes in the course of speaking about their grandparents that are not immediately relevant to the interview and yet are important and enjoyable to the respondents. Several of these are "when I was born . . ." stories relating to the adolescent's birth and the reactions of the grandparents.

Clearly grandparents are important sources of support for many of the teenagers. While some of the support is instrumental, such as a place to stay when parents are away, or gifts of money or clothing, to a large extent it is advice, or being a good listener, or doing enjoyable activities together that is important. At the same time, the importance and characteristics of the grandparent-grandchild relationship do vary.

Contrary to some previous research (Kivett, 1985), proximity affects face-to-face contact but not other kinds of contact, such as letters or phone calls, and it does not appear to affect the closeness of the relationship. Teens who live close to grandparents and those who live further away do not differ in the ways they talk about their grandparents or in the strength of their feelings. Additionally, age has little effect on the relationship, although younger adolescents have slightly more frequent face-to-face contact with grandparents than do older adolescents. This is especially true for overnight visits, particularly when the grandparents live within easy visiting distance (less than one hour driving time).

Interestingly, males are as likely as females to visit grandparents, to phone and write, to enjoy activities with them, and to express warm feelings toward them. This is somewhat surprising, considering that adult women are more likely than men to fulfill the kinship role by maintaining contact and relationships with her kin as well as her in-laws (Bahr, 1976). However, when the focus changes from frequency of contact to qualitative aspects, adolescents tend to feel closest to, and to enjoy somewhat more activities with, the same-sex grandparent. Furthermore, with a few exceptions such as the fifteen-year-old female who learned woodworking from her grandfather and the fourteen-year-old male who gardened with his grandmother, shared activities follow traditional sex-segregated lines.

Various characteristics of the grandparents affect their relations with grandchildren, although the effects are complex. At first glance adolescents are more likely to interact with, and slightly more likely to have close ties with, maternal grandparents than paternal grandparents. However, this is true only for adolescents who are living with a divorced or remarried mother. Age, education, and employment status of the grandparents have mixed effects. The least contact occurs with the oldest grandparents, who, according to grandchildren and parents, are more often in poor health, mentally incapacitated, or confined to a nursing home. However, contact is not much higher with the youngest grandparents (those under 65), who are in the best health, employed, and often involved with friends and activities of their own. The grandparents' health and the availability of alternatives to interacting with children and grandchildren are the strongest indicators of contact, findings that support those of Robertson (1977).

Why close relationships develop with some grandparents and not with others is complex. In part it is a pattern that develops when the adolescents are quite young:

> I've always been real close to my [maternal] grandma. Till I was about twelve we lived real close, so I saw her all the time. I'd stay overnight a lot, and she'd baby-sit when my mom and dad went out. (F, 16)

A close relationship is somewhat easier when the grandparent is geographically close, although proximity is not absolutely necessary:

> My husband was still in medical school when the kids were born, so we weren't living close to any of our parents. But it seemed like we saw his a lot more. We didn't travel much 'cause we didn't have a lot of money, and it was hard with two little kids. But they'd come to see us whenever they could, and my mom and dad were older and couldn't get away as easily. And sometimes, for a holiday or something special, they'd [in-laws] buy us plane tickets. So I guess the kids just knew them a lot better and were closer to them. I mean, they were close to my parents, but it was different, they knew them mostly from the phone, and getting presents in the mail. (mother of 14-year-old daughter)

The attitudes and characteristics of the particular grandparent also make a difference. At least from the perspectives of the adolescents and parents, some grandparents are more likely to take an interest in the grandchild and pursue the relationship:

> Me and my gramps always got on real well. Whenever he went fishing, he'd call my mom to see if I could go. (M, 14)

> I think my grandma just always liked having us around. It wasn't like my parents had to ask her to stay with us. Like, she'd just call and tell my mom to bring us over or leave us off for the weekend. (F, 16)

Overall, adolescents are most likely to maintain close relations with those grandparents who are emotionally available to them and make an effort to develop a close bond. Since the majority of the adolescents have a close relationship with at least one grandparent, but rarely with all of the living grandparents, grandparenthood is an achieved status in some ways. Close relationships are formed and maintained with those grandparents who actually do something to ensure that they are available to their grandchildren.

Grandparents are not only the most common relatives to be included in the adolescents' support networks, they are also the most commonly included nonparental adults. Of the 27 adolescents with at least one living grandparent, 18 name at least one as part of their support network. Three others say that they have close relationships with grandparents who currently are not able to provide support due to poor health. Of the 18, 5 include 2 grandparents as supports and 2 adolescents include 3 different grandparents. Of the 27 grandparents named as supports, 16 are grandmothers and 11 are grandfathers. The relationship with these grandparents is best characterized as a valued friendship. Common components of friendship—being a good listener, accepting the individual as he or she is, enjoying activities and spending time together—characterize the grandparent-grandchild relationship as described by the grandchildren.

ADOLESCENTS AND OTHER RELATIVES

Only four adolescents include relatives other than grandparents in their support networks. All four name at least one aunt, and one includes an uncle. Occasionally other teenagers mention aunts or uncles who are at times supportive, but clearly aunts and uncles are not common sources of support. Those adolescents who include aunts or uncles in their support networks rarely name more than two, and no one includes all of their relatives as members. Both males and females include aunts more often than uncles. In this case the adult females are in fact the "kin keepers," an effect that is not apparent in the grandparent-grandchild relationship. Quite possibly the sex effect is most important in relations that are not directly lineal.

It is not the case that some teenagers simply interact with their relatives more than other teenagers. Rather, specific aunts and uncles are supportive because of individual characteristics that are valued by the teens:

Out of all my aunts and uncles, Mary is the only one that I never called "aunt," you know, like "Aunt Mary." I guess because I never really thought of her as my aunt—she's my friend . . . like, we like the same things. I can talk to her about stuff. (F, 14)

The only one that don't think she's better than me and my mom is Aunt Jane. Me and my ma could ask her for just about anything. She was our only friend when my dad left; everybody else blamed my mom. (M, 16)

I'm not really close to my relatives. I don't think I fit in so well. But Ed [maternal uncle] I like. He's crazy about baseball. He got me in this softball league thing he does, so now we do that together every summer. (M, 17)

To some extent the parents' relationships with their siblings affect the likelihood of the adolescent's including an aunt or uncle in a support network. No teenager has initiated a relationship with an aunt or uncle who does not have a close relationship with the teen's parents, although one manages to maintain a close relationship with an aunt who has had a falling-out with the mother. While a good relationship between adult siblings helps, it is not sufficient for a supportive relationship between adolescents and their aunts or uncles. The parent-sibling relationship acts to filter out unlikely candidates, but whether a close relationship actually develops depends to a large extent on personal characteristics of the individuals involved, as in friendship.

It is notable that for several teens one of the advantages of being older is that they do not have to maintain contact with relatives they do not like or are not close to:

Last year I finally just out and told my mom I wasn't going to any of those stupid family dinners at my Uncle Dan's. Man, there isn't a one of them that knows what's going on. (M, 16)

I always felt bad about seeing my Aunt Marge because it was like she was always comparing me to Betsy [cousin], and there wasn't no way she ever thought I was as good as her. (F, 14)

I think probably my dad was hurt when once I just came out and said I didn't like Uncle John and I wouldn't go over there anymore—because, you know, it's his brother and all, and, like, I should have liked him since he was my uncle. (M, 14)

To the extent that people actively begin building their own support networks during adolescence, independently of parents, one of the first steps taken may be to remove people with whom they are not personally involved in enjoyable and supportive relationships.

Adolescents at times call upon cousins for support, but only when the cousins are very close to them in age; the cousins are almost always of the same sex. Teens may refer to particular cousins as "just like having a sister" or as "a friend." Geographical proximity is almost always necessary for such a relationship to develop. In these cases, cousins have often spent considerable time playing together and interacting as children.

Although the support provided for adolescents by relatives is limited in frequency and scope, they can be called upon for aid at some future time. That is, relatives may be inactive network members who can be drawn into active participation if the need arises. In his Northern California Community Study, Fischer (1982) finds that while kin constitute 26 percent of the people whom the respondents see socially and 48 percent of the people to whom they confide personal concerns, they constitute 67 percent of the people from whom the respondents can borrow money, which leads him to conclude that kin ties are particularly active in times of crisis. Similarly, Granovetter (1973) suggests that "weak ties" may not show up in an assessment of current sources of support but nevertheless may be useful under certain circumstances, such as finding a job. Thus, even though adolescents are not currently drawing upon their relatives for support, they may be a "reserve pool" that can be utilized in certain situations.

DIVORCE, REMARRIAGE, AND KIN: TWO HYPOTHESES

Are teenagers living with a divorced mother at a disadvantage in drawing on paternal kin? Do they receive more support from maternal kin? Does remarriage add a potential new set of kin to provide support? Empirical research bearing on these questions is sparse, but two hypotheses seem to predominate.

The Diminution Hypothesis suggests that divorce diminishes the kin network by effectively cutting off the noncustodial parents' relatives. There is some empirical support for this position. Spicer and Hampe (1975) and Anspach (1976) find that in the case of adults, contact with consanguine kin after divorce remains the same or increases, while contact with former in-laws decreases. Further, Matthews and Sprey (1984) find that maternal grandparents are in a better position than paternal grandparents to maintain contact and a close emotional relationship with grandchildren following divorce.

The Diminution Hypothesis emphasizes the importance of the child's relationship with the noncustodial parent, the assumption being that contact is more likely if the father acts as a "sponsor" for his children in relationships with his family. Unfortunately, sponsorship is rarely conceptualized clearly. In Stack's (1974) study of a lower-class black community, sponsorship is open acknowledgment of paternity by the concerned male. While the kin of a man who denies paternity can nevertheless seek interaction with the child and provide services, chances are that the lack of sponsorship deprives the child and mother of any support from the father's kin. Anspach (1976) similarly suggests that divorced fathers can serve as important links between a child and extended kin, with sponsorship operationalized as frequency of contact between the noncustodial father and his children. Children with more frequent paternal contact are more likely than children with less contact to see the father's relatives. From the grandparents' perspectives, Matthews and Sprey (1984) find that grandparents are in a better position for continued contact when their children, rather than their former children-in-law, have custody.

The Diminution Hypothesis also implies that remarriage finishes off this process by further cutting ties with former in-laws and substituting a new set of kin. However, empirical support for this idea is harder to come by. Although there is limited support (Anspach, 1976), the interpretation of findings in this area is somewhat ambiguous.

In contrast, the Augmentation Hypothesis has quite different implications for kin relations after divorce and remarriage. First, a good deal of interaction continues with former in-laws following divorce, and second, remarriage does not replace one set of kin but, rather, augments the kin network. This argument is anticipated in the perceptive essay by Bohannon (1970) on "divorce chains," in which he suggests that divorce and remarriage create complex links that span several households and draw individuals into complicated networks of spouses, ex-spouses, and so on. While Bohannon focuses on adults, a similar argument can be made regarding children.

Furstenberg (1981) takes this position in suggesting that children living with remarried parents may be in a particularly advantageous position, since a good deal of contact does occur between children and their noncustodial parents and relatives, and, furthermore, children are incorporated into the networks of their stepkin. At times the argument resembles the half-full/half-empty glass debate—how much contact is "a good deal"? Finally, focusing on the quantity of interaction obscures other, more interesting issues. It seems more profitable to focus on the process of maintaining old ties and incorporating new ties, the problems encountered and the strategies employed to cope with them, and the participants' feelings about these processes.

RELATIVES AND DIVORCE

Divorce strongly affects adolescents' interaction with paternal relatives. Interaction with relatives other than grandparents is almost nonexistent, with exceptions occurring primarily in two sets of circumstances:

> We set it up where I go for maybe two weeks every summer to my [paternal] grandparents' house to stay. And while I'm there, my grandma has sort of like a family reunion in the backyard and my two aunts and uncle and their kids and stuff come over, and we find out what everybody's done during the year and take home movies and that's it. (M, 15)

> ... when finally my mom had a job where she could keep me, my Aunt Joanne [father's sister] lived with us, and she's really the only other relative that's really important to me, even though I really only see her maybe once a year at Christmas. ... I guess you wouldn't expect for her to live with us after my mom and dad split up. But she was actually my mom's best friend. I'm not real sure about this, but it seems to me like that might be how my mom and dad got together in the first place, through my Aunt Joanne. So even after my parents divorced, she was my mom's best friend and she lived with us. (F, 16)

In the first case the paternal grandparents act as "sponsors" and arrange at least occasional contact with other relatives. In the second situation a strong friendship that existed between the mother and sister-in-law before the divorce is maintained afterward. Given that interaction between teens and their aunts and uncles in general is minimal, it is not surprising that there is even less after parental divorce.

Parental divorce also affects interaction with grandparents. Adolescents and parents both report that contact with paternal grandparents is less than it had been prior to the divorce, and considerably less when compared with contact with maternal grandparents. At times the disruption immediately follows the divorce, with virtually no contact afterward, most often when conflict is strong between the parents and when there is animosity between the custodial mother and her in-laws. In most cases interaction decreases over time, following initial attempts to maintain relations.

Reasons for decreased contact are highly complex and not always well understood by the adolescents:

I don't really know why we don't see them [paternal grandparents] anymore. It just sort of got harder and harder to go. We didn't have much to talk about, I guess. (M, 15)

At first I saw them pretty much, but, you know, it seemed like everybody just got so upset when I'd go. (F, 13)

. . . they never call me or they've never sent me birthday cards or presents or things . . . I'm not real sure [why]. It's really kind of hard for me to remember what it was like before the divorce because I was pretty young, and that was a long time ago. (F, 16)

Many factors interact in complex ways to affect the relationship between adolescents and paternal grandparents. Frequent contact with the noncustodial father makes it more likely that contact will occur with his parents, but only if he has a relatively good relationship with them; a few teens have closer relations and more frequent contact with their grandparents than with their fathers.

Identifying those circumstances which make it easier to maintain close relations with paternal grandparents is easier than identifying the factors which make it less likely. Proximity is more important for paternal grandparents than for maternal grandparents following divorce. Custodial mothers maintain close relations with their parents no matter where they live, but not with former in-laws. The further away the in-laws are, the more difficult it is to coordinate arrangements for contact between grandparents and grandchildren. It is easier if the mother has at least an amicable relationship with the grandparents. Mothers also indirectly affect the grandparent-grandchild relationship, sometimes without realizing it:

He doesn't see them [paternal grandparents] much at all anymore. I wouldn't mind if he wanted to. I never said anything to him, it just doesn't seem to matter to him much. (mother of 14-year-old son)

Her son gives a different impression:

Yeah, I'd like to see them more. I always had a pretty good time and all when I was there. But when my dad left, it just got pretty weird. I think it kind of upset my mom—like, I'd talk about her, or take my dad's side or something. She never said anything, but I think she was kind of glad when I stopped going. (M, 14)

Other teens echo this theme—the feeling that their mothers are upset by their visits with paternal grandparents, that somehow they are being disloyal to their mothers.

At times grandparents contribute to this situation. In their interviews with grandparents, Matthews and Sprey (1984) find that grandparents are poorly informed about their children's marriages. Often they are not aware of serious marital problems and sometimes are quite surprised that a divorce is being sought, at times not being told until after legal proceedings have begun. While here it is necessary to rely on the grandchildren's and parents' accounts, it appears that a similar situation prevails. At times grandparents try to use the grandchildren as sources of information about the marriage and divorce, placing the teens in an awkward position:

My dad hadn't told her [paternal grandmother] a thing, so she'd do stuff like say to me, "Well, I suppose they were fighting a lot before your dad moved out," to see if I'd agree. I never knew what to say. (F, 15)

What was I supposed to tell them? I didn't know what was going on either. (M, 16)

The grandparents' questions are often difficult for the teenagers precisely because they, too, are often uninformed about their parents' marriages or the reasons for the divorce:

I was totally blown away [upon being told of the parents' separation]. They never fought. They never did much of anything else either, but I always figured that's just the way being married was. (M, 17)

Difficulties increase when paternal grandparents actively take their child's side against the custodial mother. This occurs even when parents have made every effort to prevent the situation. These problems are most serious in the first year after the divorce, although at times they persist. One strategy for coping with this situation is to explicitly lay down guidelines for the grandparents, at times in the form of an ultimatum:

I finally told them right out that if they wanted me to keep coming over, they had to stop running down my mom. That was it. It was up to them, but I couldn't keep coming home with a sick stomach all the time from the way they talked about her. I didn't want to choose, but she's my mom, and if I had to choose, she'd win. That was it. (M, 17)

In this case the grandparents accepted the guidelines and interaction has continued. This option is most often used by the older teens who can articulate their feelings and approach their grandparents as one adult to another. Teens who do not see this strategy as an option, or who try it but fail, can either continue the unpleasant interaction with the grandparents or can cut off the interaction entirely. The predominant response is to withdraw, not initiate contact, and find excuses not to interact with the grandparents. This is not an easy option. Most of the adolescents feel quite close to their grandparents. Even when ending contact is the only, or at least the best, option, they feel sad about the choice. Some of the adolescents mourn the loss, much as they would if the grandparents had died.

Problems with relationships are not confined to paternal grandparents. Maternal grandparents, too, attempt to get information about the marriage and divorce from the adolescents, and they occasionally take sides against the father. However, maternal grandparents are at an advantage because their daughter has custody of the grandchildren, making interaction easier. First, they can avoid the stress and awkwardness of dealing with a former child-in-law to make special arrangements to see the grandchildren. Second, maternal grandparents hold privileged positions in their divorced daughters' support networks. Divorced mothers name their parents as their most important source of emotional and instrumental support, four times more than any other person. Mothers call upon their parents for help with the children as well as for money, legal advice, temporary housing, and other services. These exchanges bring grandparents and grandchildren into frequent contact, sometimes more frequent than before the divorce.

Under the difficult circumstances of divorce, the increased contact with grandparents is not always pleasurable. The three teens who have lived with grandparents until the mother could find housing and a job have discovered a new side to their grandparents:

Once I started living there, they started enforcing my curfew and all. I'd never really seen them like that. My grandpa even started suggesting I get my hair cut. (M, 17)

I guess it was pretty hard on them—I mean our moving in. It had been a pretty long time since they'd had kids around a lot, and I guess we made a lot of noise. It wasn't long before my grandma started acting just like a mom. (F, 17)

Even adolescents who have not lived with their grandparents find that they often take more responsibility for exercising authority and discipline at a time when the mothers find it difficult to do so. Furthermore, several teens are in the uncomfortable position of competing with their mothers for the attention of the grandparents:

I know the divorce was hard on my mom, and it didn't help any with him [father] running all over town with one girlfriend after another where everybody could see him. But it was hard on me, too, and I guess I just got real tired of everybody doing everything for my mom. . . . I guess that sounds pretty bad to say, but she is an adult. My grandma and grandpa would come over and bring her all this stuff and spend all their time worrying about my mom, and it was like I wasn't even there. (F, 14)

These types of problems are most common in the first year following divorce. At the time of the interviews, most of the difficulties have been worked out and grandparent-grandchild relations are close to what they had been prior to the divorce.

Paternal grandparents, however, continue to be disadvantaged in their relations with grandchildren. Relying on the accounts of grandchildren and parents precludes developing a complete explanation for lessened contact with paternal grandparents. Certainly it is not entirely the doing of the grandchildren and their mothers. Two of the adolescents who have not seen their paternal grandparents for several years have made attempts to contact them through letters. One has not received a reply after two months of waiting, and the other is still waiting after a year.

Clearly divorce changes the grandparent-grandchild relationship. Problems encountered include working out authority relations, loyalties to their own children, and feelings of anger toward the former child-in-law. By one year after the divorce most difficulties have lessened and at least maternal grandparents are able to reestablish a grandparenting relationship with their grandchildren. Paternal grandparents, however, seem particularly at risk of losing contact or, at the very least, of having lessened interaction with grandchildren.

RELATIVES AND REMARRIAGE

Thus far the evidence supports the Diminution Hypothesis of kin relations following divorce. Contact with paternal relatives does decrease following the parents' divorce. While contact with maternal kin increases, it does so temporarily and thus, in the long run, does not make up for the loss of contact with paternal kin. Furthermore, it does not seem that adolescents are incorporated into their stepfathers' networks, thereby replacing paternal kin with stepkin.

In his study of families following divorce and remarriage, Furstenberg (1981) suggests that stepkin incorporate children into their networks and children make an effort to accept stepkin, as a "stamp of approval" on their mothers' remarriage. In contrast, not one of the ten adolescents in a remarried household considers the stepfather's relatives as his or her own:

They're [stepfather's parents] not my grandparents. I mean, they're nice people and all, but they're not really related to me. (M, 13)

He's [stepfather] got three brothers, but they live all over the place, I'm not even sure exactly where. And there's only one that he really keeps in touch with, and I don't even know him very well, except to recognize his voice if he calls. (F, 16)

Relations are not unfriendly or hostile, nor do stepkin totally avoid each other. For the most part relations between the adolescents and stepkin are civil and acceptable to everyone concerned. A few adolescents have friendly relations with stepkin, visiting them occasionally with the stepfather, and sometimes exchanging birthday and Christmas cards or gifts. Relations are friendliest when adolescents have a reasonably close relationship with their stepfather and when he has a close relationship with his own relatives. But even then teens are reluctant to call stepkin "relatives." Indeed, terminology is problematic for both adolescents and parents as they attempt to describe the complex relations between those involved.

Two explanations for the contradictions with Furstenberg's (1981) results can be considered. First, all of the children interviewed here are teenagers. The ages of the children in Furstenberg's sample are not clear, although it appears that younger children are included. Whether it is easier to incorporate young children into new kin networks is in need of further study.

Second, it is possible that since Furstenberg interviewed only the adults involved, he received a different description of the situation than he would have received from the children. Consider the following accounts of relationships with stepkin given by parents and their children. The mother says:

> Well, I think that everybody has really made a big effort to fit in, and I'd have to say it's working out really well. To tell you the truth, I think the kids love it—it's like having three sets of grandparents—three times as much spoiling. (mother of 15-year-old son)

Her son has this to say:

> Yeah, I like his [stepfather] family OK, but it's kind of strange when I see them because I don't really know how I'm supposed to act or what to call them or anything. They're not really my grandparents, but I think everybody wants me to feel that way. (M, 15)

Or consider the following description of a holiday situation:

> I didn't really know what to expect when we took the kids to his parents' house for Christmas. It had me a little worried—it was our first holiday together and he had always spent Christmas there, so there was no question about it—we had to go. But when we got there, it was really nice. His parents even got them presents. I think we all had a really nice time. (mother of 16-year-old daughter)

When asked about the same holiday, her daughter provides this description:

> It was pretty bad. I mean, I know his parents are nice, but all of us together for Christmas? It was just kind of weird. His nieces and nephews were there, and when we opened presents, they had gotten coats and nice sweaters, and a radio and stuff. I got a box of stationery and my brother got socks! Can you believe that one? (F, 16)

Clearly parents overestimate the extent to which their children have been, or feel, incorporated into the new network. To some extent it is wishful thinking—all of the parents are very concerned about their children's acceptance of the new marriage, and at times minimize or even ignore the problems in order to reassure themselves that the children are adjusting. In many cases the children do their part to maintain this impression. They make efforts to be friendly with stepkin and often do not express the doubts or the hurt they feel.

Apparently the teenagers do not see acceptance of stepkin as a "stamp of approval" (Furstenberg, 1981) on the remarriage. Adolescents try to be friendly in order to avoid arguments with parents and because they are aware of their parents' wishes for everyone to get along well. At the same time, adolescents are willing and able to accept the stepfather and even have a close relationship with him, but draw the line at his relatives. Not a single adolescent includes a steprelative in his or her support network. There is no evidence to suggest that stepkin replace paternal kin after divorce and remarriage.

CONCLUSIONS

Kin, particularly grandparents, frequently provide both physical and emotional support to adolescents. In some ways this part of the social support network requires little work on the part of the adolescents, since the grandparents are virtually inherited from their parents. At the same time, adolescents are trying to establish some degree of independence from their parents. This may involve establishing some independence from the parents' support network as well, primarily by dropping relatives they are not close to. Thus, as adolescents begin constructing their own support networks, the networks are likely to decrease in size as they weed out persons who are not supportive. Adolescents in divorced families are at further risk of shrinking networks due to decreased interaction with paternal relatives. This loss is not likely to be made up for by the mother's remarriage. It is possible, however, that lost members are replaced by other people, including age-peers and nonrelated adults.

7

Adolescents and Their Friends

Social scientists as well as the mass media make much of increasing age segregation in American society (e.g., Bronfenbrenner, 1974; Elder, 1975). Presumably, adolescents especially emphasize relations with age-peers and concomitantly experience decreased interaction with adults. In fact, it has been suggested that teenagers and adults operate within quite different subcultures (Coleman, 1961), with distinct and opposing value and attitude systems.

The implications for adolescents' social support networks are twofold. First, the networks should include a relatively high number of age-peers as supports. If teenagers spend more time with age-peers, and interact within a distinct peer subculture, it is reasonable to assume that peers will be particularly important in making adolescents feel secure and "connected." Second, supportive relationships with nonparental adults are expected to be rare. Age segregation may impede interaction between adults and teenagers, making it difficult to form supportive relationships. Teenagers do, however, have regular contact with a variety of adults occupying formal roles vis-à-vis the adolescents—teachers, guidance counselors, coaches, doctors, ministers, and others. It is an open question whether adolescents see them as potentially supportive individuals, or interact with them primarily as positions.

There are many questions to consider relating to adolescents' relationships with age-peers and nonrelated adults. How important are age-peers in adolescent support networks? Do adolescents include nonrelated adults in their support networks? Are some kinds of nonrelated adults more likely than others to be included, and what kinds of support do they provide? Are siblings included in adolescents' support networks, and if so, what sorts of support do they provide? Does parents' marital status affect adolescents' relationships with age-peers, nonrelated adults, or siblings? Is the relative number of adults and age-peers in a support network related to the adolescent's well-being, communication skills, or relationship with parents?

ADOLESCENTS' FRIENDSHIPS: AGE-PEERS

Age-peers are the most frequent category of individuals in the adolescents' support networks. All 30 teenagers name at least one age-peer as a support, and three have networks composed exclusively of same-age friends. Furthermore, the adolescents name more friends in their networks than any other type of individual. On average, adolescents include a little over three age-peers in their support networks.

Friendship relationships with peers are multifaceted, with shared activities and interests being the common thread. All of the teens see their friends as providing companionship. Occasionally this includes school activities:

> Yeah, we're usually in the same classes, 'cause we're kind of doing the same sorts of stuff. We eat lunch at pretty much the same table all the time. (M, 16)

More frequently the shared activities involve extracurricular or after-school activities:

> We have some classes together. Eat together. Mostly we do stuff together after school. We might go to a football game sometimes . . . we hang out at the mall, go shopping, maybe. And weekend stuff, like maybe I'll spend the night at Maureen's house and we'll go downtown or to a movie, if nobody's having a party. (F, 15)

> We hang out. You know, after school—shoot some baskets or something. (M, 15)

Pastimes frequently shared with friends include athletics, school- or church-sponsored clubs, sporting events, spending the night at each other's house, going to parties, and "hanging out." Almost all of the adolescents "hang out" with their friends, being in the same place not so much to do anything in particular as to be around age-peers, usually in a public place, where "being seen" is a goal. The local shopping mall is by far the most popular place for "hanging out."

A majority of the adolescents also see their friends as someone to talk to:

> Yeah, we talk about stuff a lot. I guess that's most of what we do. (M, 15)

> She's real easy to talk to. I mean, we like the same stuff and go to school and stuff, so there's just a lot we talk about, you know, just the stuff we do all the time. (F, 13)

Topics discussed with friends show a good deal of variety as well as common themes:

> What else?—Guys, always guys. (F, 15)

> Oh, yeah, we talk about girls. (M, 15)

> You know, what's going on at school. Like who's hanging out with who else, or what guy invited somebody to something. You know, it's just, like, the people we know. (F, 16)

> I don't know. We talk, I guess about football and stuff. (M, 14)

> I guess we complain about our parents a lot—what they won't let us do, what pains our moms are sometimes, like, you know, what we can wear and stuff. (F, 14)

The lists are virtually endless. Most-often-mentioned themes are complaints about parents, particularly their rules and restrictions, and the opposite sex. Other age-peers and school-related matters, such as teachers, activities, or classes, are also frequent topics of conversation.

Teenagers spend a good deal of time talking to their friends. In fact, this activity is at the root of many parent-adolescent conflicts, particularly regarding time spent talking on the telephone:

> Oh, yeah, she's all the time giving me a hard time about being on the phone. I don't know why it's such a big thing with her. It's not hurting anybody. (M, 15)

> For the life of me I can't figure out what they find so much time to talk about. It's constant—she gets off from one friend and five

minutes later it's another. This goes on for hours when she gets home from school. (mother of 14-year-old daughter)

They say I see them at school, so I don't need to talk on the phone. But when do you talk? In between classes it's like five minutes. (F, 15)

This is also seen in the parents' objections to "hanging out":

He says he just talks and stuff when they're all at the mall like that. But he sees them all the time. What's there to talk about? I think it's bound to get them in trouble. They're there and there's nothing to do, so it's bound to get them into trouble. (father of 15-year-old son)

Despite having been teenagers themselves, with few exceptions parents have difficulty understanding how their teenagers can spend so much time talking to friends, especially when the topics seem rather trivial and uninteresting.

Much of the talk and interaction is of a rather casual nature, and is characterized by a joint "talking about" something rather than by mutual sharing and feedback. Slightly fewer than half (13) of the teenagers have a friendship relationship that includes mutual confiding, sharing, and self-exploration. Most of the teenagers have a "best friend," but often this simply means that they spend more time together, or talk about some things that they do not talk about with others. The 13 with close, mutual friendships, however, recognize that the *individual* is important, and are getting something personal from their relationship with that specific individual. When asked to define "best friend," they often describe some unique quality or characteristic of the person:

When I say she's my best friend, I guess I mean it's because it's different with her. There are other girls I do stuff with, but anything, like, that I really want to talk about, you know, like it's bothering me or I want somebody to really listen and, like, really tell me what they think, well, I always talk to Jan, 'cause I know she really listens and it's important to her, too. (F, 17)

He knows where I'm coming from, maybe we're a lot alike or something, but I just know whatever is going on with me, he's probably at the same place. (M, 16)

In turn, they are providing support for the friend:

She comes to me with her problems, too. She was having a pretty bad time with her mother for a while, and it was, like, well, I'm pretty sure I really helped because I'd listen to her and we'd talk about it. (F, 15)

I know there's nothing she wouldn't tell me. It's kind of an agreement that we have. We tell each other everything. (F, 16)

Clearly mutuality is a significant component of these relationships.

Another theme in these close relationships is the nonreplaceability of friends, obvious by its absence in one teenager's comparison of her friends:

Pretty much equal. Right now maybe I spend more time with Maureen. I'll go home from school and even though I just saw her, I'll call her up and we'll talk on the phone for maybe even an hour. But that sort of thing changes a lot. I mean, like right now Maureen and I do more stuff together, but this summer I spent more time with Allison, and maybe that will change next month. I mean, we're really like a group, and while sometimes we'll pair up for a while, it doesn't happen a lot. (F, 15)

This element of exchangeability is not present when the adolescents see their best friend relationships as qualitatively different from other friendships. It is the individual who is important and is providing something of himself or herself that simply cannot be given by another person.

Occasionally age-peers provide instrumental aid to each other. In fact, it is rarely mentioned spontaneously by the teens. The rather limited resources of the teens contribute, but also, most of the teens' material needs are being met relatively well by their parents. Friends loan each other money, but rarely more than the cost of a hamburger or a movie ticket. Friends, especially among the older adolescents with access to a car, help each other with transportation problems, although many younger teens have been forbidden to ride in cars driven by other teens.

Interestingly, few of the teenagers have close, exclusive other-sex relationships. Only two females and one male include a boyfriend or girlfriend as part of their support network. These relationships are close and emotionally intimate:

Yeah, she's important. I mean, would I be seeing just her if she wasn't? This is the first time I've only been seeing just one girl, 'cause it's like I don't want to see anybody else right now. (M, 17)

> We've been seeing just each other now for almost a year. It's almost
> our anniversary! There's nobody that I feel is more important to me
> right now, even my friend Ellen. If I had to choose there'd be no
> question, it'd be him. (F, 16)

These are exceptions. Four other teens are more or less seeing just one
person but are not totally closed to the idea of dating someone else if the
opportunity arises. Generally, there is a good deal of opposite-sex interaction, but it almost always takes place in a group context. This is apparent
in the following response to the question of whether the teen dates:

> No. Well, maybe. Like you go to a party and there's a lot of different
> people there. Well, you might go with all your friends, like we all go
> there together, and then you might end up standing around with one
> guy for a long time, or if you're really lucky and he's old enough, he
> might drive you home. But we don't have one guy . . . we see all the
> time. (F, 15)

The use of the plural pronoun "we" clearly captures the group essence of
other-sex interaction.

AGE, GENDER, AND PEER RELATIONS

Adolescent friendship has been conceptualized as a developmental
process that varies by age (Douvan and Adelson, 1966). Early adolescent
(ages 11–13) friendship centers on common activities, middle adolescent
(ages 14–16) friendships center almost exclusively on security and loyalty,
and late adolescent (ages 17 and above) friendship is a more shared
experience with greater emphasis on the friend's personality and interests,
and greater appreciation of individual differences. Bigelow and LaGaipa
(1975) asked children and adolescents to describe their expectations of
their best friends. They found that the dimensions of loyalty, intimacy, and
giving help appear in the descriptions for the first time between the ages
of 13 and 15.

While Douvan and Adelson's (1966) study is based almost entirely on
the reports of adolescent females, a smaller sample of boys aged 14–16
allows for some comparisons. Considerable gender differences characterize friendship expectations. Boys rarely mention sensitivity and empathy,
while common pursuits, gang activities, and the need for help when in
trouble are prominent themes (Douvan and Adelson, 1966). Furthermore,
tensions, jealousies, and conflicts between close friends are more common

themes in girls' accounts of their friendships than in boys' (Coleman, 1974). Finally, Feshbach and Sones (1971) studied the effects of a new-comer on a small group of friends, aged 14 to 15, and found that girls are less welcoming and more likely than boys to express negative or rejecting attitudes.

Age and, especially, gender differences clearly emerge in the friend-ships of the adolescents interviewed. There is an inverse relationship between age and number of peers included in the support networks. Furthermore, qualitative differences similar to those found by Douvan and Adelson (1966) are identified. Teens under 15 not only name more same-age friends but also are less likely to distinguish between them. Best friends are infrequently singled out, group experiences are emphasized, and security and loyalty are stressed. These themes are apparent in the teens' descriptions of friendship problems and conflicts:

Scott used to hang with us, but then he started going off on his own. These other guys'd ask him to play some [foot]ball or something, and he'd just go, and not tell us they were playing, so we kind of just stopped waiting around for him. (M, 13)

Well, what really bothered me was that I knew, like, they were talking about me behind my back. . . . well, like Pam would call and say, "You should have heard what Jackie just said about you," and then she'd tell me not to tell her Pam told me. And then Jackie would call and say the same thing about Pam. What a mess. I mean, that's pretty low. (F, 14)

In contrast, older teens have fewer friendships, but they are closer and more emotionally intimate.

Gender interacts with age to affect adolescent peer relations. Even the youngest girls are more likely than the boys to have a best friend. Gender differences are largest among the oldest teens, since by then almost all of the girls have a close "best friend," while boys continue to emphasize group relationships. Even boys who have a best friend rarely talk about confiding or mutual help with personal problems. Rather, being a best friend usually implies sharing somewhat more time or activities with that particular person.

ADOLESCENTS' FRIENDSHIPS: NONRELATED ADULTS

Somewhat fewer than half (13) of the teens have a supportive relation-ship with a nonrelated adult. Among these 13, the average number of nonrelated adults seen as supportive is almost three. Seven adolescents have supportive relationships with teachers, making them the most frequently mentioned nonrelated adults. Teens occasionally include athletic coaches (four), guidance counselors (three), or club or activity advisers (three), who are often teachers as well. Rarely are other professionals included in the support networks. Two adolescents include a minister, two a church-related youth group leader, two a counselor or psychologist, and one a doctor. Overall, a little over two-thirds of the supportive, nonrelated adults are individuals who relate to the adolescents at least in part through a formal role.

The remaining one-third of supportive, nonrelated adults are primarily individuals who interact with the teenagers more informally. Sometimes they are neighbors; often they are friends of the teens' parents who subsequently develop independent, supportive relationships with the adolescents:

> I think Nancy is a good friend and, yeah, she's a support. It kind of started when my mom went back to school, and she had these three friends that they all used to play cards on Friday night. They don't play anymore—two of them aren't here anymore—but I always used to hang around when they were here, and they'd talk to me and joke about stuff, and I just really liked Nancy and got pretty close to her. I think now I probably talk to her more than my mom does. (F, 16)

For those adolescents with adult friends, this kind of experience is relatively common. The adult is generally first recognized as a member of the parents' support network, and later becomes recognized as an independent member of the teen's support network. These adults are distinguished from those who are sometimes mentioned as providing some support, usually instrumental, for the teen, almost always due to their relationship with the parents. Thus, several adults are mentioned as people who might occasionally pick them up from school or keep them while the parents are away. This almost always occurs as a result of their membership in the parents' support networks.

While the majority of nonrelated adults in the support networks are teachers, most of the adolescents do not include teachers, or other professionals, in their networks. Typical is the following comment:

> . . . teachers are just teachers—you have them for a class and some are better than others, but that's about it. (F, 15)

It is obvious that simply interacting with a person occupying a formal role is not sufficient to promote other types of interaction.

Why certain teachers or other nonrelated adults actually become part of a teenager's support network is not always clear. Some hints, however, are seen in this account:

> There are two teachers that have been really important to me. . . . One was my math teacher—she moved away this year, but we write letters to each other . . . and the other is my biology teacher. . . . They started out just as teachers, but in things that I really like. I'm really good in math and science, so I really liked their classes and I always did real well in them, so I guess they liked me because of that. And I'd go in after school to ask them about homework and we'd talk, sometimes for a long time, after school. . . . I got to feel so comfortable around them that I'd talk to them about other stuff, too. Who my friends were, or if I wasn't getting along with somebody, we'd talk about that. It's just kind of strange because they're both adults and they're teachers, but that's really what I like about them. They treat me like an adult and not just like another kid. (F, 16)

Many of the adult-adolescent relationships develop in a two-step process. First, the adolescent and adult are brought together by a common interest or activity, giving them the opportunity to interact regularly. Second, interaction moves beyond the activity they have in common. Thus, with continued contact and an expanding base of common experiences, they become more aware of each other as individuals. A similar process occurs with the adults who do not occupy formal roles. In this case the impetus is not a common interest but a common person. That is, both relate to the parent and through that bond eventually come to relate to each other independently of the parent.

The kinds of support provided by nonrelated adults are of two major types. First of all, they are individuals with whom the adolescent can pursue a shared interest:

> I really like talking baseball with him [coach]. He'd drive me home sometimes from practice 'cause my house is on the way, and we'd just talk about the Braves and stuff. (M, 15)

> It turns out I'm pretty good with wood, and I wanted to make this chair, so I bought the wood and stuff, but I don't have all the tools, so Ted [teacher] said I could bring it to school and leave it there and

work on it when I wanted to after school. He's always there, so he'll help, or we'll just shoot the breeze. (M, 16)

While sometimes it is an interest that can be shared with peers or parents, often it involves a skill or expertise that requires some adult guidance which a parent cannot provide, given limited time, skill, or knowledge.

Second, nonrelated adults often act as a sounding board. Primarily this means listening to the adolescents, respecting their opinions and perspectives, and perhaps offering some advice or a new perspective. Occasionally teens talk to nonrelated adults about problems with peers or girlfriends or boyfriends, but most commonly it involves discussions about parents:

Yeah, sure, I talk about my mom to my friends, but what can they say? I mean, they're going through the same stuff, so I guess it's OK to all sit around and complain, but it's different with Joan because she's an adult and she knows my mom, so it's like she can give me her opinion and it's like it means something. (F, 15)

Uhm, I don't know what it is he [teacher] does, but it's like I'll say something about stuff at home and he really listens, and it's not like he's saying, "What d'you know? You're just a dumb kid." And he'll maybe say, like, why I think my dad did something, and it'll kind of make me think about where he's coming from. (M, 15)

By virtue of being adults, these supportive individuals can provide the teenagers with new perspectives on their parents. Most important, they do it in a casual and nonjudgmental way, making the adolescents feel as if they are being treated as adults and not as children. Indeed, when asked to describe their relationships with nonrelated adults, the refrain that is heard most often is "He/she treats me like another adult."

For a significant minority of the adolescents, support is obtained from a variety of nonrelated adults. There are no large differences by sex or age in the likelihood of having nonrelated adults in one's support network. There is a sex difference in the sense that, with very few exceptions, the nonrelated adults are the same sex as the teen. There is also a small age difference, in that older adolescents are slightly more likely to include more than one nonrelated adult.

ADOLESCENTS AND THEIR SIBLINGS

All but three of the adolescents have at least one sibling. Four teens are currently the only child living at home, leaving 23 with at least one sibling in the household. The average number of siblings is about 1.5. The average age difference between adolescents and the sibling closest in age is about two years.

Despite the availability of siblings, only six adolescents include one or more siblings in their support networks. On the surface this might suggest that the sibling relationship is not a close one, and in five cases it is not.

> She's gone to college now, so she's hardly ever here, and when she was here, we fought all the time. My mom and her get along a lot better. It seems like she always did everything my mom ever wanted her to do. What a bore. She always got good grades, and she never liked to go out and party. She never drank or . . . did stuff like that. I think kids always thought she was a real drag. I always did. I wonder what she ever did for fun. (F, 15)

> No, I wouldn't say I get support from them [brother and sister]. I mean, my sister, like, we don't do the same stuff, and Jeff is pretty much younger than me [four years], so there's not much we do. (M, 14)

Sometimes it is a matter of sibling rivalry; at other times it is simply a lack of common interests or friends.

For the six teens who do have supportive siblings, the relationship is generally close:

> Oh, yeah, Sara's [older sister] just like a friend. I mean, she's just a year older than me, so I guess we're a lot alike. And we have to share a room now since we moved, so we talk a lot. (F, 13)

> I do a lot of stuff with Tim [younger brother] 'cause we're home a lot after school and we're not supposed to go anywhere till mom gets home from work. (M, 13)

In these cases the sibling is often seen as "just like a friend." These siblings participate in joint activities, and often have friends in common. They also talk to each other about common interests or problems, including parents.

For most teens, their relationships with siblings are not so clear-cut. On the one hand, they do not see their siblings as supports, but on the other hand, their relationships are not characterized by the absence of closeness. Rather, their relationships are far more ambivalent. Many adolescents have difficulty adequately describing their sibling relationships:

It's kind of hard to say. I mean, we fight a lot. And I can't say that we, like, talk about stuff. But, you know, he's my brother, and sometimes we fool around together, and that's fun. (M, 15)

Conflict is common in the relationships, even among those adolescents with close, supportive sibling relationships. In most cases this revolves around everyday sorts of matters:

Yeah, we [he and older sister] fight a lot . . . just about stuff. I used one of her records or I changed the channel on the TV, or she's on the phone and I have to use it. (M, 14)

Do they fight? Are you kidding? Sometimes I think that's all they do. One of them can't walk into the room without another starting in on something. And I tell you, it's about the dumbest things—something one of them said, or what's on TV, or who ate the last cookie. It drives me nuts. (mother of 14-year-old daughter)

At the same time the relationship is recognized as close:

Sometimes we just sit around and talk about junk, nothing special. So it's not like we fight all the time. And even if we do, I mean, it's not like we hate each other or anything. I mean, that's just the way it is. It's not like it's a big deal or anything. (M, 15)

Indeed, for most of the teens conflict is not a "big deal"; it is a natural part of being siblings.

While variation in sibling relationships is small, a few factors tend to lead to closer sibling relationships. While there are no discernible differences in the sibling relationships of boys and girls, there is a gender effect in the sense that same-sex siblings tend to be closer, in part due to gender socialization and gender-based interests and activities. Also, about one-third of the teens share a room with a same-sex sibling. This effect is somewhat mixed, however, since sharing a bedroom gives them more opportunities for close interaction at the same time that it provides them with more opportunities to argue, often over impingements on privacy or the unauthorized use of personal possessions. Age similarity also fosters a closer relationship because it is more likely that the siblings have common interests, activities, and friends. Furthermore, sibling relationships vary by age. Older adolescents describe less overt conflict with siblings, an assessment shared by the parents. At the same time, older adolescents spend less time with their siblings. Thus, as siblings spend less time at home and more time pursuing their own interests and spending time in their own peer groups, conflict decreases, although the relationship does not necessarily become closer.

PARENTS' MARITAL STATUS AND ADOLESCENT FRIENDSHIPS

Mothers' marital status has little effect on relationships with age-peers. There are virtually no differences in the average number of age-peers in the networks of adolescents in the different household types. At the same time, adolescents currently living with a divorced mother are more likely than other adolescents to feel that their time and freedom to participate in age-peer activities are constrained by their home situation:

I have to do more stuff at home than a lot of my friends, so I probably don't get to do as much as a lot of them. Well, like my mom said I could do baseball or I could do soccer, but not both, 'cause it's too much time and she needs me to help here. (M, 14)

Yeah, I think I have a lot more responsibility. Like I can't do much of anything after school because I have to be home with Katie and Brian [younger siblings]. So maybe some of my friends are going somewhere, over to somebody's house or something, and I can't go. (F, 14)

These comments are often echoed by teens in divorced-mother households. It is a complaint common enough to make it clear that many of the teens feel somewhat deprived in their peer relations and activities. At the same time, the likelihood of including peers in the networks, the number of age-peers included, and the closeness of peer relationships do not differ noticeably between adolescents living in divorced households and those in married and remarried households. This is supported by Devall and colleagues (1986), who find that among preteens, aged 9 to 12, children in divorced households do not differ significantly from other children in their responsibilities or in the number of activities in which they are engaged. At the same time, they perceive themselves as less involved in activities than other children.

Why do adolescents in divorced households see themselves as relatively deprived, despite evidence to the contrary? Several explanations are possible. First, differences in responsibilities and activities may be qualitative rather than quantitative. Thus, if adolescents have different kinds of responsibilities, such as caring for younger siblings or cooking dinner as opposed to cleaning one's room, they may be felt as more onerous. Second, regardless of parents' marital status, teenagers are likely to view the responsibilities and activities of other teens from distorted vantage points. Why teenagers in divorced families are less accurate in their perceptions than other teens is related to a third explanation. Despite rising divorce rates, single-parent homes continue to be viewed negatively in society. Children from divorced families are likely to be aware of these negative views and thus may be more sensitive to small differences between themselves and other children, and may be more likely to blame them on the divorce. At this point, the only conclusion that can be drawn is that adolescents in divorced families manage to maintain peer relationships that, at least on the surface, are very similar to those of teens who apparently have more time for doing so.

Mother's marital status does have an impact on sibling relationships. Leupnitz (1982) notes that sibling relationships tend to change after parental divorce, with younger children fighting more after the divorce and older siblings getting along better. The evidence here suggests that sibling relationships are closer when the mother is divorced, a difference that continues after she remarries. Of the six teens who include siblings in their support networks, four live with a divorced mother and the other two live with a remarried mother. Even those teens who do not see their siblings as supportive describe more joint activities, more time spent together, and, overall, more talking and sharing. In part this is due to the shared experience of coping with the parents' divorce:

> It hit us all pretty hard when they ended up finally splitting. I guess we should have known it was coming, but I guess you never really think they'll go through with it. So when they did, it helped to kind of talk about it, and we all, I guess, just felt better 'cause it wasn't like I was the only one it was happening to. (M, 17)

In part it is due to the increased responsibilities placed on the teens and the increased need for cooperation:

> Mom expects certain things to get done by the time she's home from work, so if we don't cooperate and we just spend our time arguing about stuff, then it doesn't get done and we're all in for it. (F, 14)

It's like we're a team. We all gotta pull together or else stuff just won't get done, so I think we get along pretty good. (M, 13)

Also, due to divorced mothers' work or school schedules, the children often spend more time at home together, with only each other to talk to:

> You know, I think they've really gotten closer. We have a rule, since I have to be out one or two nights a week, the only way I let them stay by themselves is if they're both here and nobody else comes over. So they pretty much have to rely on each other to talk to and do things. So Matt's showing Scott how to use his computer, or the other night they cleaned up the basement and I didn't even tell them to! (mother of 13-year-old son)

Clearly, sibling relationships are closer when the mother is divorced. Furthermore, sibling relationships in remarried households are more similar to those in divorced households than to those in married households. Once a cooperative and close sibling relationship is established, it tends to continue.

The most substantial impact of mother's marital status is on relationships with nonrelated adults. Only one teen in a married household includes any nonrelated adults in the support network. Seven of the teens living with a divorced mother include at least one nonrelated adult, as do five of the teens living with a remarried mother.

There are several possible explanations for these differences. One is that teens living with a divorced mother are exposed to a larger number and greater variety of adults than teens living with both parents, since divorced mothers have larger and more varied networks of their own. One divorced mother describes her support network in this way:

> You should have come on a Saturday—it's an absolute madhouse! That's when we do everything around the house that needs to get done, and mostly, I have to admit, it's stuff my husband probably would have done . . . before, but I'm just learning, so sometimes there are probably 10 or 12 different people here doing something or showing me how to. . . . OK, like Saturday, Carol, next door, was helping me plant roses; two guys from my divorced people's group were working on my car; my brother and one of his friends were putting up wallpaper in the bathroom; Jan, a friend from work, came over because I want to learn how to make quilts and she said she'd

teach me; and, gosh, I don't know, I'm sure there was somebody else. I mean, it really is a madhouse. (mother of 14-year-old daughter)

While this is extreme, it is not unusual for divorced mothers to rely on a broader group of people to provide the aid and support that very often comes only from a husband prior to divorce. After remarriage, some of this effect diminishes because there is once again a husband who can provide a great deal of support. However, several remarried mothers note that one lesson learned from their first marriage and divorce is not to become dependent on one person to meet their needs. Thus, remarried mothers, on average, have support networks whose sizes fall between those of divorced mothers and married mothers.

Adolescents in married households are exposed to adults as well, but often the circumstances are very different. Usually the parents interact with other adults on a social basis, going to dinner with them, playing cards or bowling, or having them over for the evening. These activities are highly age-segregated, with children rarely included. If they are too young to be left at home alone, a baby-sitter is used. Even entertaining at home usually involves attempts to minimize intrusions by the children—giving them dinner early or restricting them to certain rooms.

Not only are teens in divorced homes exposed to a wider variety of adults, they are exposed to and included in many adult activities, often from young ages. Due to limitations on time, mobility, and money, divorced mothers often take their children with them to social functions and other adult activities that they probably would not take them to under ordinary circumstances. Thus, many teens are very used to interacting with adults and feel very comfortable doing so. Increased early interaction with adults, their particularly close relationships with their mothers, and their added responsibilities all contribute to better communication skills and increased maturity, as indicated by their comfort with the interview situation, their ability to answer the questions, and their openness with the interviewer. Thus, not only are these adolescents more comfortable interacting with adults, it is possible that adults find them easier to interact with.

CONSEQUENCES OF AGE-PEER AND NONRELATED ADULT FRIENDSHIPS

The relative inclusion and exclusion of age-peers and nonrelated adults in adolescent support networks may have various consequences. Relations with parents, communication skills, and overall well-being may all be affected. None of these outcomes are measured using standardized tests or scales, so much of this discussion is suggestive rather than conclusive.

Do parents and peers compete with each other for adolescents' loyalties? Actually, rather than competing, they may be complementary, in that the relative influence of each depends upon the situation in question (Brittain, 1968; Larsen, 1972a, 1972b). Also, there is a good deal of value similarity between age-peers and adults (Troll and Bengtson, 1979). Furthermore, the answer may depend on how competition is defined. There is little indication here that close relationships with age-peers preclude close relationships with parents. In fact, those adolescents with the closest parental relationships, largely those who are living with a divorced mother, also have the closest relationships with age-peers. There may in fact be certain skills, abilities, and attitudes that lend themselves to forming close, intimate relationships, whether with age-peers, parents, or other adults.

To some extent evidence suggests that parents and peers are in fact complementary in the support provided. Peers provide minimal instrumental support for each other, since most parents are better able and more willing to provide this for their adolescent children. When emotional support is considered, differences between parents and peers emerge in the kinds of things that are talked about:

> I'd feel sort of funny talking to my mom about guys. I mean, I guess
> I could, but things were pretty different when she was dating and it's
> just, well, with my friends it's all that we ever talk about. (F, 15)

Teens commonly feel that they can talk to peers, but not to parents, about relationships with the other sex, sexuality in general, alcohol, and drugs. When parents are talked to, it is usually for factual information rather than to discuss one's own, or friends', feelings and experiences. This is the largest difference between peers and parents. Parents are also more likely to be consulted about matters pertaining to the teen's future. Among the older teens there is an increasing awareness of life after high school, and most discuss the issue of college and its alternatives with their parents, while friends rarely discuss it, except in the abstract.

Despite the possibility of close relationships with both, and the seeming complementarity of the relationships, there are conflicts that arise between adolescents and their parents concerning peers. Rarely is the *choice* of friends an issue. Very few teens feel that their parents disapprove of their friends, a view corroborated by the parents. According to both parents and adolescents, adolescents choose friends quite similar to themselves in family background, social class, and neighborhood.

The most likely source of conflict is the amount of time spent with friends. Furthermore, the concern is often not about the influence of peers but the feeling that much of this time can be spent on more valuable pursuits:

> She's doing well in school—mostly Bs and an occasional C, but what really bugs me is that I think she's really capable of doing better, and I really think she would if she spent half the time she spends talking on the phone on her homework. (mother of 16-year-old daughter)

The complaint is fairly common. Parents feel that the adolescents have only so much time, so time spent with friends cannot be spent on other pursuits, such as reading, homework, or other school-related activities.

There are other peer-related concerns expressed by parents, but many are more abstract and not necessarily focused on their children's friends per se:

> You pick up the paper now and it seems like every day there's something in there about drug problems at the high school. And, yeah, I worry about it. Scott starts there next year, and you just can't ever be sure what'll happen when they're exposed to that kind of stuff, no matter what you've told them and how you've raised them. (mother of 15-year-old son)

Drugs, alcohol, and sex are almost universal concerns among parents. While some are concerned that their child might get in with the "wrong crowd," most parents see these as pervasive problems, not confined to "bad" teenagers.

Overall, parents do not compete with peers, except perhaps in the amount of time spent on peer-related versus other activities. It is very possible simultaneously to maintain close, supportive relationships with both parents and peers. Peer support is complemented by parents, who are more likely to be sources of instrumental support and are more likely to be sources of information, particularly regarding future plans and decisions. Parents and adolescents do at times come into conflict over peer-related issues, but rarely is it directly related to the adolescent's friends. Rather, the concerns revolve around the time spent in peer activities or issues seen as almost universal problems with teenagers, such as alcohol and drugs.

Similar questions can be raised about relationships with nonrelated adults. First, age-peers and nonrelated adults may compete with each other for inclusion in support networks. Adolescents who include nonrelated adults differ only slightly from other adolescents in the average number of age-peers who are included—about 2.5 for those who include non-related adults, compared with just slightly over 3 for those who do not. The largest difference is qualitative. Teens who have supportive relationships with nonrelated adults are more likely than other teens to have a "best friend," to have closer, more open relationships with all of their friends, and to relate to them more as individuals than as a group with interchangeable parts. Thus, teens who draw on nonrelated adults have larger support networks because these individuals are additional, not substitute, members of their support networks. Furthermore, these teens have a wider variety of supportive relationships and are more likely to relate to network members as unique individuals, regardless of whether they are age-peers or adults, related or nonrelated.

It is also possible that nonrelated adults compete with parents, or even replace them, in adolescent support networks. All but three of the teens include at least one parent in their network, and among those who do not, none include nonrelated adults. Furthermore, the adolescents who are most likely to include nonrelated adults in their networks are those who have the closest relationships with their mother. If anything, rather than competing with mothers, relationships with nonrelated adults may actually improve the relationship by providing the teen with an adult perspective on the relationship and relieving some of the burden on the mother.

Those teens who are most likely to draw on nonrelated adults for support are adolescents living with a divorced mother. Thus, the possibility remains that nonrelated adults compensate for the father's absence. Once again the evidence suggests otherwise. While boys are more likely to draw on men, girls are more likely to draw on women for support. Furthermore, teens describe their relationships with nonrelated adults as far more similar to their relationships with friends than with parents. If the father's absence affects the likelihood of including nonrelated adults in one's support network, it is probably an indirect effect. The absence of a father promotes a closer relationship between mother and adolescent, which in turn makes it more likely that an adolescent will draw on nonrelated adults for support.

How network structure affects well-being is a crucial but complex question. Well-being is examined only directly and subjectively. When asked how satisfied they are with their lives and whether they would like to change anything, most teens would change some things, but the majority are quite content. Furthermore, satisfaction varies little by mother's marital status or network structure. Teens who have nonrelated adults in their networks appear to have the best communication skills and to be the most mature, and to have the closest relationships with their mother. The direction of influence is an open question. While interacting with non-related adults certainly improves teenagers' communication skills and perhaps relieves mothers of some of the burdens of dealing with a teenager, it appears that a close relationship with the mother comes first, following from changes in the household following the parents' divorce. The question of exactly what impact network structure has on the well-being or other characteristics of adolescents is a question open to further investigation.

CONCLUSIONS

Age-peers are clearly important sources of support for most adolescents. They are the most commonly mentioned, and there are more of them in the networks than any other kind of person. Possibly the negative aspects of adolescent peer relations have been exaggerated. Significantly, contrary to the expectation of competition between parents and peers, those teens with the closest relationships with parents are also the teens with the closest relationships with age-peers. Siblings are rarely seen as supportive, although sibling relationships are generally close, despite a good deal of conflict. A significant minority of adolescents have supportive relationships with nonrelated adults. These adults either begin interacting with the teens in a professional role and go on to develop supportive relationships, or are first members of the parents' support network who come to be recognized as independent members of the adolescent's network.

While these relationships vary by the age and sex of the adolescent, the largest effect is related to mother's marital status, with teens in divorced households having the most distinct relationships. The least impact is seen on peer relations, where, despite time constraints and increased home responsibilities, and contrary to their own perceptions, adolescents in divorced-mother households maintain relations quite similar to those of other teens. Sibling relationships are closer when the mother is divorced, due in part to the greater need for cooperation in the household and the increased time siblings often spend together. The largest difference is in the area of support from nonrelated adults, who are included most often when the mother is currently divorced, followed by when the mother is currently remarried. Teens in these situations have often been exposed to, and have interacted with, a large number and variety of nonrelated adults, often from relatively young ages. Due to this and their greater communication skills, related to their close relationships with their mothers, these adolescents feel comfortable interacting with adults and often draw on them as sources of support.

8

Implications for Adolescents

Adolescents are traversing a life stage characterized by ambiguity and ambivalence in American society. They are continually reminded of their impending adulthood but are given few opportunities to practice adult behaviors. They are encouraged to be independent at the same time they remain economically, physically, and emotionally dependent upon their parents. They are told to think for themselves while being ensconced in a peer group on whose opinions and evaluations their self-concepts often rest. Further complicating this picture is the fact that increasing numbers of adolescents are facing or have already faced the dissolution of their parents' marriage and the likely remarriage of at least one of their parents. Clearly the potential for instability and flux is tremendous.

As a resource, social support networks may provide adolescents with some degree of stability. Weathering life transitions, whether universal, like adolescence, or unpredicted, as in parental divorce or remarriage, may be easier if one has supportive relationships on which to depend. Of course, the situation is actually much more complex. Adolescence as a life stage and parental divorce and remarriage are life events that are quite likely to disrupt social support networks. Conflicts with parents over responsibilities and rights may make it difficult to rely upon them for emotional support. Furthermore, divorce and remarriage may negatively affect parent-child relationships as well as disrupt relationships with other support network members, such as grandparents. Furthermore, American society is highly age-segregated, providing adolescents with limited opportunities to interact with adults outside their families.

Despite the obvious potential for negative consequences, most teenagers survive adolescence. Furthermore, while the evidence is less conclusive, it also appears that the majority of children who experience parental divorce and remarriage eventually manage to weather that transition. To what extent adolescent social support networks are affected by parental divorce or remarriage, and to what extent support networks mitigate potential negative outcomes of these transitions, are open questions.

This research has been an attempt to develop at least tentative answers to these questions. Several focal concerns have guided the research and will be reconsidered in light of the empirical findings. Finally, the implications for future research and theory development will be discussed.

WHAT DO ADOLESCENT SOCIAL SUPPORT NETWORKS LOOK LIKE?

As predicted, adolescent social support networks are heavily populated by parents and age-peers. Age-peers are clearly the most common sources of support, being named by all 30 of the adolescents. There is a good deal of variability in the types of support provided by age-peers, with joint activities and having someone to talk to being most common. Instrumental support from friends is minimal, consisting largely of loaning small amounts of money, trading clothes, and providing transportation. Fewer than half of the adolescents have a friendship with an age-peer that includes mutual sharing and confiding. Particularly among the younger teens, a "best friend" is defined quantitatively rather than qualitatively, as someone who is seen more often or with whom one shares more joint activities compared with other friends.

Overall, there is a high degree of fluidity and exchangeability in the age-peer segment of adolescent support networks. Younger teenagers in particular see their friends as a group, do not draw distinctions between them, and are reluctant to name a "best friend." On the other hand, older teenagers have fewer friends but are closer to the ones they have and are more likely to view and value them as individuals. Drawing developmental conclusions from cross-sectional data is questionable at best. At the same time, documented age differences should remind us that adolescence spans several years, so it is quite likely that adolescent friendships will change over time. Young adolescents are just beginning to assert their independence from parents, and with the entry into junior high school are moving into a new social arena where clique membership and friendships are likely to be in a constant state of flux. As they approach adulthood, older adolescents begin dealing with the issue of intimacy in both same- and other-sex relationships, and become more concerned with the quality of individual friendships.

The issue of whether peers or parents are more important as sources of support is complex, and depends in part on how importance is conceptualized. Parents are less likely to be included in adolescent support networks than are age-peers, but only slightly. However, of the 27 adolescents who include parents as well as age-peers in their networks, all have at least one age-peer friendship that they consider to be as close as, or closer than, their relationships with parents. At the same time, relationships with parents are more multifaceted, with parents providing a greater variety of support than is obtained from age-peers. Besides their economic and residential ties, parents and adolescents are bound together by a history. Thus, even when the relationship is characterized largely by conflict, parents and adolescents recognize their continuing interdependence.

In further considering the significance of parents as supports, a major qualification is in order. It is necessary to distinguish between mothers and fathers before drawing any meaningful conclusions about parents' network roles. Fathers, even those who share a residence with their child, are less likely to be named as sources of support, and to provide fewer and different types of support compared with mothers. Fathers are authority figures, provide economic support, and at times share joint leisure activities with their children, while mothers provide a variety of instrumental supports, such as lending money, chauffeuring, and doing household maintenance chores; deal with everyday needs and problems; act as go-betweens for adolescents and fathers; and serve as confidantes.

The division of labor between mothers and fathers is part of a more general division of labor between females and males in American society: women are expected to nurture and men to provide. In the family context this means that mothers carry the burden of everyday child care while men fulfill their parental roles more indirectly, by providing for their families economically. While it is certainly possible that changing gender roles will involve men more directly in nurturing relationships with their children, it is likely that change will be slow. Indeed, none of the kinds of support provided by fathers is likely to lead to particularly close relationships between them and their children. Authority figures and economic providers often act from a distance, and at least the former role is likely to engender resentment and fear rather than closeness. Even those fathers who share leisure activities with their adolescents have only recently begun to do so, and are likely to be doing it, at least in part, as a way of relieving mothers of some of their burdens.

For several reasons, there is less overt conflict between adolescents and fathers than between adolescents and mothers. First, while fathers make rules and decisions, mothers are often left to enforce them. Second, mothers actively shield fathers from a good deal of conflict by taking care of minor problems themselves. Finally, it may be very difficult, if not impossible, for people to develop a close, intimate relationship without experiencing conflict. It is in the context of continually dealing with everyday needs, problems, and conflicts that mothers and adolescents develop close, mutually binding relationships.

Only two types of people besides parents and age-peers are even moderately likely to be significant sources of support. Grandparents are common sources of support for their adolescent grandchildren. They often form relationships that are best described as close friendships, character-ized by a high degree of closeness and mutuality. The second type of person at times found in adolescent support networks is nonrelated adults. Over-all, the likelihood of drawing on nonrelated adults for support is not very high. When nonrelated adults are included, they are most commonly school personnel.

In general, adolescent social support networks are smaller than adult networks. Additionally, adolescents look almost exclusively to two spheres for supportive relationships. In the context of their families, adolescents remain highly dependent upon their parents and also develop close rela-tionships with grandparents, and occasionally with other relatives as well. In the context of school, adolescents form numerous supportive relation-ships with age-peers and come into contact with a variety of potentially supportive school personnel who occupy formal roles. As adolescents age, it is expected that their support networks will undergo both quantitative and qualitative changes. As adolescents become more independent, it is expected that their social worlds will expand and their networks will become more diverse in membership. Furthermore, as they begin forming families of their own and settle into long-term occupational roles, it is assumed that their networks will include more people with whom they have particularly close, mutual, and multifaceted relationships.

HOW ARE ADOLESCENT NETWORKS AFFECTED BY PARENTAL DIVORCE OR REMARRIAGE?

Adolescents living with a divorced or remarried mother have social support networks that differ substantially from those of adolescents living with both of their biological parents. Divorce diminishes the supportive role of fathers at the same time it qualitatively changes the mother-adoles-cent relationship. These changes have significant ramifications throughout the support networks. Divorced fathers are at a decided disadvantage. No matter how it is measured, the divorced father-adolescent relationship is less close and more problematic than relationships between adolescents and custodial mothers and fathers. The amount of contact between divorced fathers and their children is low, and it decreases over time. Contact is easier when fathers are geographically close, but proximity is no guarantee of more frequent interaction. Furthermore, compared with custodial fathers, divorced fathers have more difficulty establishing and maintaining clear roles for themselves. They are seldom significant economic providers and are much less likely to be authority figures. Divorced fathers often fall back on the stereotypical "weekend father" role, showering their children with gifts and treats, and shepherding them from one amusement to another, a role that becomes more difficult as children grow older.

Changes in the father-adolescent relationship after divorce also have impacts on other network segments, particularly relationships with paternal kin. Contact between paternal grandparents and their grandchildren declines substantially following divorce, and interaction becomes more problematic. Geographical proximity is especially important for paternal grandparents after divorce—the farther away the paternal grandparents, the less frequent the interaction. Fathers can act as "sponsors" for their children, so that adolescents who have more frequent contact with the divorced father are more likely to have continued contact with his parents. However, this is the case only when the father has a close relationship with his parents. While mothers rarely actively prevent their children from seeing their grandparents, they can make it more difficult and uncomfortable for them to maintain a close relationship. Teenagers whose mothers are not altogether happy about the continuing influence of their former in-laws may find it easier to withdraw from the grandparental relationship and discontinue interaction.

Contact with other paternal relatives is almost nonexistent following parental divorce. Even divorced fathers who actively seek to maintain contact between their children and parents rarely do so with siblings or other kin. In fact, paternal grandparents who stay in touch are more likely than fathers are to "sponsor" the children with other relatives, making efforts to arrange get-togethers when grandchildren are visiting and acting as clearinghouses for family news. Not only, then, are grandparents important sources of support themselves; they are also important links to other supports.

Clearly, parental divorce has potentially devastating consequences for adolescent social support networks, and this at a time when adolescents are most in need of support. While fathers may not be central members in adolescent support networks prior to divorce, after divorce their membership becomes even more problematic and the likelihood that they will drop out altogether increases. Significantly, if they do move to the fringes or drop out, they are likely to take others, particularly grandparents, with them. At the same time, it is possible that these losses are at least partially compensated for by changes in other segments of the networks. Thus, qualitative changes in the mother-adolescent relationship are the second distinguishing facet of adolescent support networks after parental divorce.

Contrary to expectations, while divorced mothers face considerable problems not faced by others—overload, economic difficulties, loneliness—the problems often lead to closer mother-adolescent relationships rather than more problematic ones. In coping with their problems, divorced mothers often rely on their children in ways they would not were the husband present. Age and sex barriers that lead to greater parent-children segregation in married households are broken down, and consequently divorced mothers and their children relate to each other on more equal footing. While divorced mothers form particularly close relationships with their children, this is not the case for divorced fathers without custody. Divorced mothers are not only likely to be confidantes for their teenagers, they are also likely to call upon their children as confidants, a situation that rarely, if ever, arises when the parents are married. In contrast, divorced fathers are not seen as confidants by their children, nor, from the teens' perspectives, are fathers likely to confide in their children.

Changes in the mother-adolescent relationship after divorce have implications for other parts of the networks. Interaction with maternal grandparents following divorce is somewhat easier than it is with paternal grandparents, and in many cases increases in frequency because divorced mothers' most important post-divorce supports are their parents. At the same time, increased interaction with maternal grandparents is not always pleasant. Teenagers at times feel that their grandparents' attention is in many cases focused on their mothers in an effort to meet their instrumental and emotional needs. Furthermore, given that grandparents are often uninformed about their children's marriages and the reasons for divorce, they at times attempt to get information from the adolescents, placing them in awkward and uncomfortable positions. As the initial problems subside, however, maternal grandparent-grandchild relationships return to their pre-divorce states. Compared with paternal grandparents, maternal grandparents are able to maintain relatively high degrees of contact with their grandchildren.

The divorced mother-adolescent relationship also has an indirect effect on the structure of adolescent social support networks. Adolescents in married households are highly unlikely to include nonrelated adults in their support networks. However, almost three-quarters of the adolescents living with a divorced mother and half of those living with a remarried mother include at least one nonrelated adult—on average, they include three such adults. The majority of these adults, particularly teachers and other school personnel, begin interacting with the adolescents in formal roles and then go on to develop more informal and individualized relationships that arise out of a common interest or joint activity.

The fact that supportive relationships with nonrelated adults are especially likely when the mother is currently divorced or has been divorced, raises the question of exactly what it is about living in a divorced-mother home that predisposes teenagers to form supportive relationships with such adults. One possibility is that adolescents attempt to replace the noncustodial father with nonrelated adults. For two reasons, this explanation is unlikely. First, it is not clear why adolescents in such circumstances would seek out individuals to whom they are not related. Theoretically, relatives can act in this capacity but, with the exception of grandparents, interaction with relatives is minimal and, in fact, decreases after divorce. Second, if it is the noncustodial father who is being replaced, one would expect the replacements to be predominantly males. This, however, is not the case. With respect to relatives, aunts are more likely than uncles to be included by both girls and boys in adolescent support networks. In the case of nonrelated adult supports, boys are more likely to turn to adult males, and girls are more likely to turn to females.

It seems more likely that certain conditions arising out of early situations in divorced-mother households, as well as particular facets of the divorced mother-adolescent relationship, place adolescents in a position where it is not only possible, but likely, that they will develop supportive relationships with nonrelated adults. For one thing, due to overload, limited money, and restricted social lives, divorced mothers often bring their children into interaction with a variety of adults at relatively young ages, and actively incorporate them into adult social activities. Furthermore, due to their close relationships with their mothers, teens living in divorced-mother homes develop strong communication skills. Thus, as a result of their earlier experiences and greater ease in communication, they are more comfortable interacting with adults and are in a better position to develop supportive relationships with nonrelated adults.

One area in which the mother's marital status has a very limited impact is in the age-peer segment of the support networks. Contrary to expectations, there are no differences by mother's marital status in the likelihood of including age-peers or in the average number included. Despite the fact that adolescents in single-parent homes complain about greater limitations on their time and freedom due to greater family responsibilities, they are actually not disadvantaged in terms of the number of friendships they are able to maintain. In fact, those teens with the closest relationships with their mothers—the teenagers in divorced families—turn out to have the closest relationships with age-peers. They are more likely to describe their friends as individuals and to include mutual sharing and confiding as important aspects of their relationship. At the same time, it is possible that adolescents compensate for problematic parental relationships by drawing more heavily on age-peers for support. Among the three adolescents with support networks composed entirely of age-peers, two are living in divorced-mother households and one is living in a married household. All three have highly conflictual relationships with their custodial parent. It appears that the quality of the parent-adolescent relationship is at least as important as parents' marital status.

The mother's remarriage following divorce leads to further shifts in adolescent social support networks. The particularly close divorced mother-adolescent dyad conflicts with the prevalent notion in American society that the marital dyad should predominate over the parent-child dyad. In most first marriages the couple relationship develops prior to the children's births, giving the couple time to establish their relationship as the primary dyad. This situation is reversed in remarriages involving children from previous marriages. Thus, the mother-child relationship is not only established first, it is particularly close due to the circumstances of the divorce and living in a single-parent household. Most mothers subscribe to the value of the primacy of the marital dyad and therefore withdraw somewhat from their children, spending less time alone with them and confiding in them less, particularly about matters relating to the stepfather. This is an especially difficult situation for adolescents, who have to adjust not only to a new stepfather but also to a changed relationship with their mother.

The mother's remarriage also affects father-adolescent relationships, but the outcomes are more complex and less consistent. Overall, jealousy and competition between biological fathers and stepfathers are common problems that persist even several years after the remarriage. Adolescents deal with the competition and the need to incorporate the stepfather into the family system in a number of ways. Most commonly, they work out substantively different, but satisfying, relationships with both their biological father and their stepfather. This outcome is more likely when the biological father is close and interaction is fairly frequent and satisfying. When one is chosen over the other, more teens draw closer to the stepfather and withdraw from the biological father than vice versa (three as opposed to one). This outcome is especially likely when interaction with the biological father is very infrequent or when the relationship is not particularly pleasant. Stepfathers who are able to negotiate the most mutually satisfying relationships with their stepchildren are those who do not force themselves into stereotypical "father" roles but interact with their step-children as individuals.

Little evidence is found to support the claim by some (Furstenberg and Spanier, 1984) that children are incorporated into the kin networks of their stepfathers, thereby providing them with an additional set of relatives. While younger children may in fact be "adopted" by stepkin, it is a more difficult process for adolescents, who do not share a history with stepkin. Additionally, in general many adolescents have begun to withdraw from active interaction with their biological kin as they begin to assert their independence and establish relationships outside their families. Furthermore, adolescents apparently do not feel compelled to accept stepkin as relatives in order to show their approval of either their stepfather or their mother's remarriage. Most are able to maintain a satisfactory relationship with the stepfather without recognizing his relatives as their own. This is very apparent in the difficulty adolescents have in finding appropriate terms to denote steprelatives.

Adolescent social support networks are clearly sensitive to changes in the mother's marital status. Mothers and fathers play different but very important roles in the support networks of their children, both directly and indirectly. Their divorce has significant ramifications for their relationships with their children as well as throughout their children's support networks. Quantitative as well as qualitative changes occur in adolescent support networks due to parental divorce. The likelihood of including certain types of people, the kinds of support that are provided, and the characteristics of the relationships are all sensitive to the type of household in which an adolescent is living.

HOW DO NETWORK SIZE AND STRUCTURE
AFFECT ADOLESCENT WELL-BEING?

Determining the "supportiveness" of adolescent networks is difficult. All of the teenagers are relatively satisfied with their lives and feel there is not much they would change if given the chance. At the same time, about one-fourth (eight) of the adolescents say they often feel lonely. Feelings of loneliness do not vary with age, although slightly more boys (five) than girls (three) frequently feel lonely. In addition to these subjective self-assessments of well-being, adolescents vary in their ability to formulate clear strategies for solving problems and their willingness to call upon people in their support networks. It is assumed that large, varied networks can provide more types of support and can ensure that if some members are unable to provide support in a given situation, there will be other members who can step in and offer support.

Size in and of itself turns out to be a relatively insignificant aspect of adolescent support networks. Having a relatively large network does not prevent one from feeling lonely, nor does it guarantee that members will be able to meet the adolescent's needs. At the same time, size is not entirely irrelevant. The largest networks tend to include the greatest variety of members, and it is this characteristic of membership diversity that is most important in making adolescents feel their support networks can be relied upon. The more diverse the network membership, the more likely it is that adolescents can formulate clear solutions to a number of problems, and the more likely they are to explicitly mention drawing on their support networks for doing so. Thus, for example, when asked what they do if they need to borrow a small sum of money or they want clothes they cannot afford, adolescents with relatively large, diverse networks can come up with a variety of strategies, often drawing on network members for help. Several suggest that they can go to specific individuals in their networks for money; others say they can exchange their labor or other favors for money from network members. On the other hand, adolescents with smaller, more homogeneous networks are more likely to say they do not know what they would do or that they would do without whatever it is they want. Networks composed of relatively homogeneous members— largely age-peers or almost exclusively family members—are redundant in the kinds of aid they can provide.

One of the most significant aspects of adolescent social support networks, particularly in decreasing feelings of loneliness, is the inclusion of at least one member with whom the adolescent has a close, mutual, sharing relationship. The teenagers who are least likely to feel lonely are those who include a close confidant among the members of their networks. Regardless of network size or membership diversity, if even one confidant is included, feelings of loneliness are effectively guarded against.

It appears, then, that if the criteria are emotional supportiveness and dependability in meeting one's needs, the network configuration that best fits the needs of adolescents is one which includes a wide variety of members, at least one of whom is a close confidant. The adolescents who are most likely to have networks of this type are those living with a divorced mother. They are especially likely to include a variety of adults in their networks and to have closer, more mutual relationships with the members. When asked what they most like about their teenagers, divorced mothers are more likely than other mothers to mention their children's independence and their sensitivity. Married parents are more variable in their responses and often mention personality characteristics or abilities, such as intelligence, creativity, or "outgoingness."

Does this mean that adolescents are better off when their parents are divorced? Not necessarily, although it does raise serious questions about the assumptions underlying the presumed links between household type, network configuration, and adolescent well-being. Living in a household with a divorced mother is *different* from living in a household with married parents or with a remarried mother and a stepfather. To ask if one type of household is better than another, however, distorts our vision. Currently in American society all three of these household types, as well as others, are common. Theoretically and practically it makes more sense to focus on how household members deal with the different kinds of problems and issues they face, and what kinds of resources are most helpful under differing sets of circumstances.

Likewise, if the question is what kind of adolescent network is best, the reply has to be, best for what? Teenagers are likely to face numerous demands, problems, and contingencies throughout adolescence, some of which are related to their parents' marital status and others of which are not. In the process of dealing with these circumstances, support networks are constructed, maintained, and reconstructed. Living in a certain type of household is likely to influence network size and structure by influencing the number and kinds of people, resources, and situations to which one is exposed. Network size and structure, in turn, affect one's ability to cope with those situations. In other words, network building is a dynamic process, and network structure and coping are reciprocally related.

IMPLICATIONS FOR RESEARCH AND THEORY

This research raises at least as many questions as it answers. Much more information is needed concerning the ways in which adolescent support network members are recruited. Living with a divorced mother is one situation that predisposes adolescents to incorporate nonrelated adults into their networks. There is a need to identify other circumstances that might have similar consequences. Specifically, with regard to parental divorce and remarriage, several questions arise concerning network recruitment. The strategies by which adolescents negotiate relationships between their biological fathers and stepfathers need to be examined more carefully.

Indeed, little is known about the circumstances under which stepkin relationships in general are developed. Finally, more rigorous research is needed on the links between adolescent social support networks and well-being.

Tentative answers have been offered for some of the more pertinent questions relevant to the support networks of adolescents and the ways in which they are affected by family environment. Theoretically, several conclusions are warranted. First, it is critically important to conceptualize families as *systems* of interaction. What goes on in one segment of a family is likely to have repercussions in all other segments. In American society certain norms prevail concerning the marital dyad. For instance, it is to be established prior to the coming of children, it is to be segregated from other family members, it is to involve mutual sharing and confiding, and so on. What is often ignored is that defining the marital dyad in this way has impacts throughout the family, such as in parent-child interaction. Consequently, varying the marital dyad norms, as is done in divorced or remarried households, affects the entire family and the interaction that goes on within it.

Second, as they are currently conceptualized and measured, social support networks are relatively static phenomena. What is needed in conceptualization, research design, and analysis is an explicit recognition of the dynamic process by which support networks are constructed and reconstructed. Network building does not stop once a particular outcome is reached. Support networks change in size, structure, and effectiveness throughout the life cycle.

Finally, given the tremendous variety in family forms prevalent in American society, it is necessary to stop using the nuclear family as a measuring rod against which all other types of families are compared. Focusing on what divorced families lack, compared with married households, provides a highly distorted view of what life in such families is like. More attention should be paid to identifying the strategies various kinds of families use to cope with their life situations, and those conditions which affect their use and effectiveness. Empirically and theoretically, our understanding of the workings of families will continue to be limited until there is explicit recognition of the viability of diverse family forms.

Appendix: Methodology
and Interview Schedules

TALKING WITH ADOLESCENTS AND THEIR PARENTS

Semi-structured, in-depth interviews were conducted with 30 adolescents and their custodial parents between December 1982 and January 1984. Since the research was exploratory in nature and the intent was to obtain detailed information on adolescents' support networks, broad, open-ended questions were used in order to give respondents as much latitude as possible in answering, rather than forcing answers into objective categories based on a priori judgments concerning what support is or who provides it. Due to the time and energy required to conduct this type of interview, the sample size was necessarily restricted. Thus, questions concerning the frequency of the patterns found or the generalizability of the findings to a larger population are left largely unanswered. However, fairly easily discernible patterns began emerging after just a few interviews were completed in each group. By the time all interviews were completed, it was clear that there are commonalities in the adolescents' experiences at the same time there are individual variations and peculiarities.

Potential participants were obtained through word-of-mouth contacts with friends, colleagues, a high school teacher, and a minister, and had to meet three criteria for inclusion. First, the teenager had to be living with both biological parents in a first marriage, or with a divorced mother who had not remarried, or with a divorced mother and stepfather. Compared with death, after divorce the potential for interaction with the absent parent remains but is complicated because of a separation in physical space, and possibly strained relations between the parents. Contact with others, including relatives, also may be affected by divorce and remarriage in ways that do not occur following death. For these reasons, adolescents living with a widowed parent were excluded from the sample. In addition, parents had to have been divorced for at least two years. Hetherington and colleagues (1979) suggest that the first two years following a divorce are the most difficult; after this time most families have returned to a normal routine. Ideally a longitudinal research design could be used to see how support networks are immediately affected, how they are utilized to cope with divorce and remarriage, and whether there are long-term changes in the support networks following divorce and remarriage. Given limited resources, and since interest lies primarily in the implications of living with a divorced or remarried parent, rather than adjustment to divorce and remarriage per se, only families past the initial adjustment period were included.

Second, potential respondents had to be between the ages of 13 and 17. It is assumed that teenagers have greater potential than younger children for making their own contacts and building their own support networks, due to their greater mobility and independence from their parents. At the same time, it is not expected that this is a homogeneous age group. An effort was made to include a diversity of teens covering the whole age range, in order to explore age variations.

Finally, the sample was restricted to whites, leaving questions concerning racial variations in support networks unanswered. This is unfortunate, since the experience of living with a divorced mother is more common for black children than for whites (Cherlin, 1981), and there is evidence that blacks have more varied and active support networks than whites (Stack, 1974). However, the primary concern is with the effects of parents' marital status rather than other factors, such as race. Thus, it is felt that this restriction is legitimate.

The initial word-of-mouth effort yielded eight contacts, six of whom met all the criteria for eligibility. The parents of these six adolescents were contacted by telephone and were told that I was interested in interviewing teenagers about their relationships with age-peers and close adults, including parents. They were also told that if their child participated, I would want to interview the parents as well. Five parents gave permission for their children to be contacted. The one who refused cited lack of time and hectic schedules as the reasons for refusing. The five teenagers were then contacted by phone, and all five consented to an interview.

A snowball sampling design was used to obtain subsequent participants. At the end of each interview, the adolescent was asked for the names of friends he or she thought might participate. Parents also were asked for the names of families they knew with at least one adolescent in the home. If it was determined that the criteria for inclusion were met, the adolescents were contacted.

If the purpose of a study is to draw generalizations about a larger population, a random sample is preferred. However, if one draws a random sample of children in a particular area, chances are that the proportion of the sample who live in one-parent households will be small. It is possible to draw a sample of all children with a divorced parent from county court records, but court records include only persons who have obtained a divorce in that particular county. Persons moving to the county after obtaining a divorce elsewhere will be excluded, biasing the sample in favor of people who are geographically immobile following divorce. The problems are exacerbated if one wants a random sample of adolescents living with a stepparent. For all of these reasons a nonrandom sample has been employed.

It was decided that the group of adolescents in each of the three living arrangements should be of equal size, each containing ten. The category of adolescents living with both biological parents in a first marriage was filled first. Finding suitable participants for the study slowed down considerably at this point. There was a high degree of redundancy, wherein many of the contacts made could not be used because the category already had reached its quota and a participant of a very particular type was needed, such as a fourteen-year-old boy living with a divorced mother and stepfather. Thus, the time invested was yielding fewer and fewer usable contacts. Presumably this would be a problem anytime a researcher is attempting to fill certain categories, some of which are more common than others. In order to fill the other two categories, several participants were recontacted for additional names. Further, instead of asking teens for the names of their friends, they were asked if they knew of anyone who met more specific criteria, such as living with a divorced mother or having a stepfather in the home. Eventually the sampling technique yielded a total of 30 adolescents and their custodial parents, equal numbers of whom are situated in each of the three living arrangements under consideration.

The snowball sample design turned out to have a built-in advantage. Particularly in the cases of age and sex, and to a slightly lesser degree in the case of social class, teenagers choose friends quite similar to themselves. The consequence is that asking the teenagers for contacts yielded three groups of adolescents quite similar to each other along the dimensions of age, sex, and social class. Thus, comparisons of the support networks by parents' marital status can be made with more confidence because the groups are similar on additional factors that might affect support networks.

One problem with the snowball sampling strategy relates to the nature of adolescents' peer relations. Younger adolescents, approximately under the age of 15, were reluctant to supply names when asked for contacts. Typical responses were "I don't think my friends would like it if I gave you their names" (14-year-old female), "I think I'd better ask them first" (15-year-old female), or "Why don't I kind of bring it up to them, and if they say OK, it'll be all right" (14-year-old male). On the other hand, parents willingly supplied, on the average, the names of two or three families. Those who did not give any contacts generally said they did not know any families that met the specifications. The older adolescents, those 15 or older, showed a different pattern. They willingly supplied the name of their "best friend" but then were unable to provide additional names, insisting that they did not really have any other friends. This is a particularly difficult problem for the snowball design, since if adolescent A names B as a best friend, B is likely to name A as a best friend. Thus, the sampling process stops there, with neither participant able to provide additional contacts.

These patterns present methodological problems for the researcher, but they also lend support to research on adolescent friendships. Friendship is a developmental process that takes different forms and serves varying functions at different ages (Bigelow and LaGaipa, 1975; Douvan and Adelson, 1966). Douvan and Adelson (1966) find that among middle adolescents (ages 14–16 in their sample), the dimensions of friendship stressed almost exclusively are security and loyalty, with friendships in this age group particularly vulnerable to jealousy, insecurity, and fears of disloyalty. The unwillingness of the younger teens to furnish friends' names can be interpreted as an attempt to remain loyal to them, hence the response "I'll have to check with them first," which is not found among the older teens or adults. Furthermore, Douvan and Adelson (1966) suggest that while younger teens are more likely to have several friends, to be in groups or cliques, and to have more fluid or changeable friendship choices, older teens are more likely to have one "best friend," a choice that does not fluctuate much. Again this is supported by the older teens' insistence that they really have only one very good friend. There are no strong sex differences in either of these patterns, although the patterns are somewhat stronger among girls than boys.

Particularly if one is interested in adolescent friendships or peer relations, it makes sense to be cognizant of these patterns and either to work around them or to accommodate them in the research design, in sampling as well as in subsequent stages. With younger teenagers, some type of group contact, where all of the clique members are approached together, may be more appropriate than contacting them individually, thereby avoiding any appearance of undermining the group's trust or loyalties.

The majority of the participants were interviewed in their homes, although a few were seen either in my office or at the interviewee's workplace. Every effort was made to conduct interviews in private. In some cases adolescents and parents were interviewed in one visit to the home, but in the majority it was necessary to make two or three appointments in order to interview all the parties. All adolescent interviews were tape-recorded. Interviews ranged from 45 minutes to 2.5 hours, averaging about 1.5 hours. Parent's interviews were considerably shorter, with mothers' averaging about 50 minutes in length and fathers' averaging about 25 minutes. Parental interviews covered less material than the adolescent interviews, so it is understandable that they were shorter. However, fathers' interviews on average were considerably shorter than mothers', despite their being asked basically the same questions. Fathers were more reluctant to be interviewed and were not as cooperative, being more likely to cancel appointments, almost always the last family member to be interviewed, and overall less comfortable during interviews. The only two participants to refuse to be tape-recorded were a father and a stepfather.

The major line of questioning in adolescent interviews focused on sources of support. Desired information included the adolescent's understandings of what support is, who provides it, and a detailed description of the adolescent's relationship with each network member, including how particular individuals provide support, how frequently they are seen, what kinds of things they do together, how close the adolescent feels to them, and how much conflict they experience. In addition, adolescents were asked to compare the people in their networks with each other along the dimensions of support provided, closeness, conflict, and so on. Comparisons were used to determine whether specialization was occurring in the support networks, that is, whether some kinds of people were more likely than others to be providing certain kinds of support, or whether everyone in the network was providing relatively similar kinds of support.

Probes were used to determine whether there were additional sources of support left off the list for some reason. Adolescents were asked specifically about their relationships with relatives, especially grandparents, stepkin, neighbors, ministers, teachers, counselors, baby-sitters, and other such persons who might provide support. An attempt was also made to ascertain why they had been excluded from the original list. One last attempt was made to identify additional supports by presenting adolescents with several hypothetical situations, such as needing a small amount of money or wanting advice about dating, and asking them to describe how they would handle each one. Finally, adolescents were asked about satisfaction with their lives, changes they would like to make, and feelings of loneliness, in order to make some assessment of the adequacy and impact of the support networks.

In the cases of adolescents in divorced or remarried households, a second major line of questioning concerned their feelings about their parents' divorce or the subsequent remarriage of their mother. Relevant information included initial reactions and adjustments, the effects of the divorce or remarriage on relationships with their mother, and assessments of their current relationships with the noncustodial biological father and the stepfather. Questions concerning the noncustodial father and stepfather were included even if they were not mentioned in the original list of sources of support. Questions covered how often the father is seen, when the visits occur, other kinds of contact (such as phone calls), changes in their relationship since the divorce or remarriage, and satisfaction with the relationship. Questions concerning the stepfather were much the same as those asked about the biological parents, but additionally covered early adjustment to the stepparent, problems encountered, and how, if at all, they have been resolved.

Interviews with parents were intended to do three things. First, parents' views on their relationships with their adolescents were wanted, including how much time they spend together, what activities they share, assessments of how much and how well they communicate, and the amount of conflict between them. Second, information similar to that obtained from the adolescents was desired concerning the parents' support networks, including who provides support, frequency of contact, kinds of support provided, and closeness of the relationship. Third, in the cases of divorced or remarried parents, background information on the divorce and remarriage was needed, including the length of time since the divorce or remarriage, ages of the children when the events occurred, custody and visitation arrangements and subsequent geographical mobility, as well as more subjective assessments of the children's reactions to the divorce and remarriage, and subsequent changes in the mother-child relationship. Also, while adolescents were being interviewed, parents filled out a brief questionnaire dealing with background information on the family, including education, income, ages of all children in the home, and length of residence in the community.

Interview schedules were pretested with two teenagers and two parents. No major problems were detected in either schedule, although minor rewording was done to make the questions shorter and simpler. Furthermore, the ordering of the questions on the parents' schedule was changed so that interviews began with questions concerning the support networks rather than the relationship with the adolescent. This ordering put the respondents more at ease, particularly if the parent-adolescent relationship was conflictual. Overall, it was determined that the questions were clear, were relatively easy to answer, and yielded meaningful and insightful answers.

The exact ordering of the questions as well as the wording varied somewhat from one respondent to the next, depending on their understanding of the questions, their interests, and the topics that they brought up in the course of the interview. However, every effort was made to ensure that the same topics were covered and the same information was obtained from each participant. Items were checked off on the interview schedule as they were covered and, whenever necessary, the respondents were recontacted if certain needed information was missing.

No major problems were encountered while conducting the interviews, although interviewing several members of the same family at times can raise minor problems. At the time of the initial contact, parents were told that the adolescents' interviews concerned relations with age-peers and adults, including parents. Adolescents were told that their parents were being interviewed as well. In all cases the adolescents were interviewed before the parents. Thus, the problems encountered varied somewhat between the adolescents and the parents.

Adolescents were assured at the time of the initial contact, as well as at the time of the interview, that their responses were completely confidential. However, given the nature of the questions and the fact that parents were being interviewed, many of the adolescents initially were hesitant about at least some of the questions, making rapport particularly difficult to establish. The order in which topics were covered became especially important. Beginning with relatively safe topics, particularly ones that respondents enjoy talking about, such as friends, helps to relieve some of the initial anxiety felt by many of the teenagers. Furthermore, difficult topics, or matters about which adolescents appear hesitant to be open, can be backed away from and tried from a somewhat different angle later in the interview, when interviewees are more comfortable.

Parents present two different problems. First, at some point in the interview, most parents expressed some interest in or curiosity about what their children had said. This was usually subtle, as in the case of the mother who began her response with "I suppose he told you . . . ," and then looked at the interviewer for confirmation. Under these circumstances interviewers must be particularly careful to remain neutral and to make it absolutely clear to the respondent that the child's answers are confidential. When this is done firmly and consistently, parents are cooperative and do not force the issue.

A second, more interesting problem arises when the parent's interview directly contradicts the adolescent's interview. This arises both in subjective interpretations of events or relationships and in objective reports on such things as the frequency of visits with a noncustodial parent or the length of time since the last contact with a parent or other relative. There are at least two ways in which to interpret and use these differences. For one, it is possible to look at the interviews as a sort of validity check on the information received. Thus, discrepancies in this case are interpreted as errors on the part of one of the respondents. The task for the interviewer in this case involves determining which account, if either, is relatively more accurate. One way to do this is to recontact the respondents in order to determine whether they misunderstood the question, or whether there is some other clear explanation for the discrepancy.

However, a second interpretation is viable. That is, it is possible that even though the parents and adolescent share the same household, they do not necessarily have the same experiences, nor do they necessarily interpret the same event or relationship from a similar perspective. In this case, the interviewer's task is not to reduce or resolve the discrepancies, but to determine the factors that are responsible for them. This interpretation would seem more reasonable when the discrepancies concern relatively subjective matters, such as the closeness of a relationship. Furthermore, there may be relatively objective matters for which either the parent or the adolescent has a better vantage point from which to view them. For example, parents might have a more accurate view of how custody and visitation arrangements were negotiated, whereas adolescents may have more accurate views of how visits with noncustodial parents are spent. At the same time, even apparently objective phenomena can appear different when viewed from varying perspectives. Thus, perhaps the greatest advantage of interviewing multiple members of the same family is that this is the only way one is likely to identify and understand the differing viewpoints of the members, thereby getting a fuller and more varied picture of the family and its relationships.

Data management began almost simultaneously with the first completed interview. With the exception of one father and one stepfather who refused, all of the interviews were tape-recorded. To protect the anonymity of the participants, their names were not included on the tapes. Each family was given an identification number, and the list of identification numbers and names was kept only until the interviewing process was completed. The tapes were transcribed by the interviewer as soon as possible after the interview, and only the identification number was put on the transcript. Each adolescent's interview transcript was kept with the parents' transcripts and questionnaire in a separate file folder.

Multiple copies of each of the transcripts were made to facilitate the data analysis phase. Analysis of the transcripts proceeded almost simultaneously with data collection. After each tape was transcribed, notations concerning interesting ideas, questions, or theoretical insights were made in the margin. When approximately one-fourth of the interviews had been completed, transcript copies were cut into pieces and sorted into file folders with other related pieces of the interviews. Originally, transcript pieces were sorted by the individuals providing support, for example, parents, peers, or teachers, as well as by the kind of support being provided, such as instrumental or emotional support. As the process of interviewing and transcribing proceeded, additional folders were set up concerning relations with steprelatives, conflicts with parents, and other substantive topics that seemed relevant and interesting. Multiple copies facilitated filing pieces of the interviews into several different folders if they were relevant. As the interviews were coming to a close, the folders were organized into a general outline. The same was done with the pieces of the interviews within each folder.

The data analysis process in this instance is emergent, in the sense that analysis categories emerge from the data and inform subsequent interviews. These interviews then provide tests for the developing hypotheses that lead to revisions in the hypotheses, and so on. This contrasts with the more traditional method favored by quantitative social scientists, whereby hypotheses are formulated prior to data collection, and analysis does not proceed until data collection is completed. Data are then analyzed in such a way as to explicitly test the hypotheses. With the strategy used here, data collection and analysis proceed almost simultaneously and inform each other, a strategy most useful when the research is largely exploratory.

INTERVIEW SCHEDULES

Adolescent Interview Schedule

Name

Sex

Age

Grade in school

  School attended

Ages and sexes of siblings

Everyone has certain people who are important to them—people who help us with our problems or give us support.

  Can you tell me who the people are who give you support?

What kind of support do they give you?

How often do you see them?

What kinds of things do you do together?

Do they ever give you gifts, or help you out by giving you things or doing things for you?

How often do you argue?

  Do you have any other kinds of problems with this person?

How long have you known each of these people?

How close are you to your mother/father?

  What do you mean by "close"?

  How does your closeness compare with the other people who give you support?

How often do you argue with your mother/father?

  What do you mean by "argue"? What are these arguments like?

What kinds of things do you argue about?

How are arguments resolved? How do they end?

Has your relationship with your mother changed since your mother's divorce/remarriage?

How satisfied are you with your relationship with your mother/father?

Do you feel not close enough, or too close?

Are you satisfied with the time you spend together?

What changes would you like to make?

How well do your parents understand you?

How close do you feel to your (noncustodial) father?

How often do you see him?

How long do your visits last?

What kinds of things do you do when you visit?

How satisfied are you with your visits with your father?

Do you talk on the phone, write letters, or have other kinds of contact with your father?

How often do you argue with your father?

What kinds of things do you argue about?

How are arguments resolved?

How has your relationship with your father changed since your parents' divorce?

How has your relationship with your father changed since your mother's remarriage?

How satisfied are you with your relationship with your father?

Do you feel close enough, or too close?

What changes would you like to make in your relationship?

How well does your father understand you?

Has your father remarried?

How close do you feel to your stepfather?

Did you have trouble adjusting to your stepfather, or has that gone pretty well?

What do you call him?

Are there things you have done to try to get along better with him, or to get closer to him?

How often do you argue with your stepfather?

What kinds of things do you argue about?

How are arguments resolved?

How satisfied are you with your relationship with your stepfather?

Do you feel close enough, or too close?

Are you satisfied with the time you spend together?

Are there changes you would like to make in your relationship with your stepfather?

How well does your stepfather understand you?

How close do you feel to each of your brothers and sisters?

What kinds of things do you do together?

Do you have any friends in common?

How often do you argue with each of your brothers and sisters?

What kinds of things do you argue about?

How are arguments resolved?

Do you talk about your problems with your brothers or sisters?

Have you talked about your parents' divorce with your brothers or sisters?

Have you talked about your mother's remarriage with your brothers or sisters?

Who are your closest friends?

How long have you known each of them?

How did you meet each of them?

How much time do you and your friends spend together?

What kinds of things do you and your friends do together?

Do all of your friends know each other?

What kinds of things do you talk to each of your friends about?

Are there things you don't talk to any of your friends about?

How often do you argue with each of your friends?

What kinds of things do you argue about?

How are arguments resolved?

Do you have any other kinds of problems with any of your friends?

Do you date anyone?

Do you have relatives you feel close to?

How are you related?

Do they live nearby?

How close do you feel to each of them?

How often do you see each of your relatives?

Do you talk on the phone, write letters, or have other kinds of contact with your relatives?

Do you receive gifts from any of these relatives?

Do any of these relatives give you things or do things for you to help you out?

Have your relationships with any of these relatives changed since your parents' divorce?

Have your relationships with any of these relatives changed since your mother's remarriage?

How satisfied are you with your relationships with each of these relatives?

How close are you to your stepfather's relatives?

Did you have any problems accepting his family, or has that gone pretty well?

Did his family have any problems accepting you?

Are there any problems between your different sets of relatives?

Do you ever feel like you have too many relatives?

Is there anyone else we haven't talked about yet who gives you support?

Do you get support from any teachers? ministers? sitters? housekeepers? doctors?

I'm going to describe a few situations or problems for you. You may have experienced some of them, but regardless of whether you have or not, I'd like you to tell me how you would handle each of them.

(a) You want new clothes you can't afford.
(b) You failed a test in school.
(c) You had an argument with one of your parents.
(d) You need to borrow ten dollars.
(e) You feel kind of down and need someone to talk to.
(f) You need some advice about dating.

Do you think your life has changed much since your parents got divorced?

Do you think your life has changed much since your mother got remarried?

Is there anything about your life you'd like to change?

Do you ever feel lonely?

Overall, how happy would you say you are?

Are there any people or activities that are important to you that haven't come up yet?

Parent Interview Schedule

Are there people (besides your spouse) that you rely on for help with your children or other aspects of your life?

How long have you known each of these people?

What kinds of support do they provide?

How often do you see each of these people?

How often do you argue with each of these people?

What kinds of things do you argue about?

How are these arguments resolved?

Some people might give us support by just being friends—someone to do things with or just talk to. Is there anyone who gives you support in this way?

What do you mean by "support"?

How often do you see each of these people?

What kinds of things do you do together?

What kinds of things do you talk about?

Are there things you wouldn't talk about with any of these people?

How often do you argue with each of these people?

What kinds of things do you argue about?

How are these arguments resolved?

Are there any other people who help you, either by doing things for you or by being a friend?

Do you get support from any ministers? neighbors? family friends? coworkers? housekeepers? sitters? relatives?

Are there any relatives that you feel close to?

How are you related to each of these people?

Do they live close by?

How close do you feel to each of these relatives?

How often do you see each of these relatives?

How often do you talk on the phone?

Do you write letters or have other kinds of contact?

Do any of these relatives give you gifts, give you things, or do things for you to help you out?

How often do you argue with each of these relatives?

What kinds of things do you argue about?

How are arguments resolved?

Have your relationships with any of your relatives changed since your divorce?

Have your relationships with any of your relatives changed since your remarriage?

How satisfied are you with your relationships with your relatives?

Do you consider your ex-spouse's kin your relatives?

How often do you see your former in-laws?

Do you talk on the phone, write letters, or have other kinds of contact?

Did you have any problems with your former in-laws before the divorce?

Have you had any problems with your former in-laws since your divorce?

What are your children's relationships with your former in-laws like?

Do they visit?

Do they have other kinds of contact?

How close would you say they are?

Do you consider your (new) spouse's kin your relatives?

How often do you see your (new) husband's relatives?

Do you have other kinds of contact with them?

What do you call them?

Were there any problems with you or your children being accepted as part of your (new) husband's family?

How were the problems handled?

How are holidays and vacations arranged?

Whom do the children spend them with?

I'd like to talk for a little while about your relationship with your (target) child. Overall, how close would you say you feel to him or her?

How much time do you spend together?

What kinds of things do you do together?

Do you eat meals together?

Do you and your child talk about your own or your child's problems?

Are there things you don't talk about with your child?

How often do you and your child argue?

What kinds of things do you argue about?

How are arguments resolved?

Compare your relationship with (target) with your relationship with your other children.

Compare your relationship with (target) with his or her relationship with his or her father/stepfather.

Has your relationship with (target) changed since your divorce?

Has your relationship with (target) changed since your remarriage?

Overall, how satisfied are you with your relationship with (target)?

What changes would you like to make?

How were custody, visitation, and child-support arrangements made?

Have they changed since the divorce?

Have they changed since your remarriage?

How well do you get along with your ex-spouse now?

How often do you see him?

Are visits cordial, or not?

Do you talk on the phone or have other kinds of contact?

How often do you argue with your ex-spouse?

What kinds of things do you argue about?

How are arguments resolved?

Has your relationship with your ex-spouse changed since your remarriage?

Has your ex-spouse remarried?

Has his remarriage affected your relationship?

How would you say your children get along with your ex-spouse?

How often do they see him?

Do they have any other kinds of contact with him?

How close do you think they are?

How well would you say your children get along with their stepfather?

Have there been problems adjusting since the remarriage?

What kinds of things have you done to deal with or minimize the problems?

Are there things you would do differently, given the opportunity?

I'm going to describe a few situations or problems for you, some of which you may have experienced. For each one describe how you would go about handling it.

(a) You would like to send your child to summer camp but can't afford it.

(b) Your child is failing a course required to graduate.

(c) You find out that your child is periodically skipping school.

(d) You want to go away for the weekend and need someone to keep the children.

(e) Your car breaks down and you need someone to pick up your children from school every day for a week.

(f) You need to borrow your rent money until you get paid.

(g) You had a really rotten day and you'd just like to talk to someone.

Do you think your life has changed much since your divorce?

Do you think your life has changed much since you remarried?

Is there anything about your life that you would like to change?

Do you ever feel lonely?

Overall, how happy are you?

Are there any people or activities that are important to you that haven't come up yet?

Bibliography

Acock, A. C., D. Barker, and V. L. Bengtson. 1982. "Mother's Employment and Parent-Youth Similarity." *Journal of Marriage and the Family* 44(2): 441–455.

Acock, A. C., and V. L. Bengtson. 1980. "Socialization and Attribution Processes: Actual vs. Perceived Similarity Among Parents and Youth." *Journal of Marriage and the Family* 42(3): 519–530.

Amato, P. R. 1987. "Family Processes in One-Parent, Stepparent, and Intact Families: The Child's Point of View." *Journal of Marriage and the Family* 49(2): 327–337.

Ambert, A. M. 1984. "Longitudinal Changes in Children's Behavior Toward Custodial Parents." *Journal of Marriage and the Family* 46(2): 463–467.

Ambert, A. M. 1986. "Being a Stepparent: Live-in and Visiting Stepchildren." *Journal of Marriage and the Family* 48(4): 795–804.

Anspach, D. 1976. "Kinship and Divorce." *Journal of Marriage and the Family* 38(2): 323–330.

Asp, E., and J. Garbarino. 1983. "Social Support Networks and the Schools." In J. K. Whittaker, J. Garbarino, et al. (eds.), *Social Support Networks: Informal Helping in the Human Services*. New York: Aldine.

Bahr, H. M. 1976. "The Kinship Role." In F. I. Nye (ed.), *Role Structure and Analysis of the Family*. Beverly Hills, CA: Sage.

Baranowski, M. D. 1982. "Grandparent-Adolescent Relations: Beyond the Nuclear Family." *Adolescence* 17: 575–584.

Barranti, C. C. R. 1985. "The Grandparent/Grandchild Relationship: Family Resource in an Era of Voluntary Bonds." *Family Relations* 34(3): 343–352.

Bengtson, V. L., and J. A. Kuypers. 1971. "Generational Differences and the Developmental Stake." *Aging and Human Development* 2: 249–260.

Berman, W. H., and D. C. Turk. 1981. "Adaptation to Divorce: Problems and Coping Strategies." *Journal of Marriage and the Family* 43(1): 179–189.

Bernard, J. 1956. *Remarriage: A Study of Marriage*. New York: Dryden Press.

Bigelow, B. J., and J. J. LaGaipa. 1975. "Children's Written Descriptions of Friendship." *Developmental Psychology* 4: 178–181.

Bittman, S. J., and S. R. Zalk. 1978. *Expectant Fathers*. New York: Hawthorne Books.

Bohannon, P. 1970. "Divorce Chains, Households of Remarriage, and Multiple Divorces." In P. Bohannon (ed.), *Divorce and After*. Garden City, NY: Doubleday.

Bohannon, P. 1979. *Stepfathers as Parents*. DHEW Publication No. (ADM) 79-815. U.S. Dept. of Health, Education, and Welfare. Washington, DC: U.S. Government Printing Office.

Bott, E. 1971. *Family and Social Network*. 2nd ed. London: Tavistock.

Bowen, G. L., and D. K. Orthner. 1986. "Single Parents in the U.S. Air Force." *Family Relations* 35(1): 45–52.

Bowerman, C., and D. Irish. 1962. "Some Relationships of Stepchildren to Their Parents." *Marriage and Family Living* 24: 113–121.

Bowman, M. E., and C. R. Ahrons. 1985. "Impact of Legal Custody Status on Fathers' Parenting Postdivorce." *Journal of Marriage and the Family* 47(2): 481–488.

Brand, E., and W. G. Clingempeel. 1987. "Interdependencies of Marital and Stepparent-Stepchild Relationships and Children's Psychological Adjustment: Research Findings and Clinical Implications." *Family Relations* 36(2): 140–145.

Brandwein, R. A., C. A. Brown, and E. M. Fox. 1974. "Women and Children Last: The Social Situation of Divorced Mothers and Their Families." *Journal of Marriage and the Family* 36(3): 498–514.

Brittain, C. V. 1968. "An Exploration of the Bases of Peer-Compliance and Parent-Compliance in Adolescence." *Adolescence* 2: 445–458.

Brittain, C. V. 1969. "A Comparison of Rural and Urban Adolescents with Respect to Peer vs. Parent Compliance." *Adolescence* 3: 59–68.

Bronfenbrenner, U. 1974. "The Origins of Alienation." *Scientific American* 231: 53–61.

Cherlin, A. J. 1978. "Remarriage as an Incomplete Institution." *American Journal of Sociology* 84(3): 634–650.

Cherlin, A. J. 1981. *Marriage Divorce Remarriage*. Cambridge, MA: Harvard University Press.

Cherlin, A. J., and J. McCarthy. 1985. "Remarried Couple Households: Data from the June 1980 Current Population Survey." *Journal of Marriage and the Family* 47(1): 23–30.

Christensen, L., and D. McDonald. 1976. "Effect of a Support System on Single-Parent Families." *Psychology* 13(3): 68–70.

Clingempeel, W. G., and E. Brand. 1985. "Quasi-Kin Relationships, Structural Complexity, and Marital Quality in Stepfamilies: A Replication, Extension, and Clinical Implications." *Family Relations* 34(3): 401–409.

Clingempeel, W. G., E. Brand, and R. Ievoli. 1984. "Stepparent Relationships in Stepmother and Stepfather Families: A Multimethod Study." *Family Relations* 33(3): 425–432.

Coleman, J. C. 1974. *Relationships in Adolescence*. Boston: Routledge and Kegan Paul.

Coleman, J. C. 1980. *The Nature of Adolescence*. London: Methuen.

Coleman, J. S. 1961. *The Adolescent Society*. New York: The Free Press.

Coleman, M., and L. Ganong. 1987. "An Evaluation of the Stepfamily Self-Help Literature for Children and Adolescents." *Family Relations* 36(1): 61–65.

Colletta, N. D. 1979. "Support Systems After Divorce: Incidence and Impact." *Journal of Marriage and the Family* 41(4): 837–846.

Davis, K. 1940. "The Sociology of Parent-Youth Conflict." *American Sociological Review* 5: 523–535.

Devall, E., Z. Stoneman, and G. Brody. 1986. "The Impact of Divorce and Maternal Employment on Pre-Adolescent Children." *Family Relations* 35(1): 153–159.

Douvan, E., and J. Adelson. 1966. *The Adolescent Experience*. New York: John Wiley.

Duberman, L. 1975. *The Reconstituted Family: A Study of Remarried Couples and Their Children*. Chicago: Nelson-Hall.

Eggebeen, D., and P. Uhlenberg. 1985. "Changes in the Organization of Men's Lives: 1960–1980." *Family Relations* 34(2): 251–257.

Elder, G. H. 1975. "Adolescence in the Life Cycle: An Introduction." In S. E. Dragastin and G. H. Elder (eds.), *Adolescence in the Life Cycle*. New York: John Wiley.

Erikson, E. H. 1968. *Identity, Youth and Crisis*. New York: W. W. Norton.

Fast, I., and A. C. Cain. 1966. "The Step-Parent Role: Potential for Disturbances in Family Functioning." *American Journal of Orthopsychiatry* 36(3): 485–491.

Fein, R. A. 1978. "Research on Fathering: Social Policy and an Emergent Perspective." *Journal of Social Issues* 34(1): 122–135.

Feshbach, N., and G. Sones. 1971. "Sex Differences in Adolescent Reactions Towards Newcomers." *Developmental Psychology* 4: 381–386.

Fine, M. A. 1986. "Perceptions of Stepparents: Variation in Stereotypes as a Function of Current Family Structure." *Journal of Marriage and the Family* 48(3): 537–543.

Fischer, C. S. 1982. *To Dwell Among Friends: Personal Networks in Town and City*. Chicago: University of Chicago Press.

Furstenberg, F. F., Jr. 1981. "Remarriage and Intergenerational Relations." In R. W. Fogel, E. Hatfield, S. B. Kiesler, and E. Shanas (eds.), *Aging: Stability and Change in the Family*. New York: Academic Press.

Furstenberg, F. F., Jr., and C. W. Nord. 1985. "Parenting Apart: Patterns of Childrearing After Marital Disruption." *Journal of Marriage and the Family* 47(4): 893–904.

Furstenberg, F. F., Jr., C. W. Nord, J. L. Peterson, and N. Zill. 1983. "The Life Course of Children of Divorce: Marital Disruption and Parental Contact." *American Sociological Review* 48(5): 656–668.

Furstenberg, F. F., Jr., and G. B. Spanier. 1984. *Recycling the Family: Remarriage After Divorce*. Beverly Hills, CA: Sage.

Ganong, L. H., and M. Coleman. 1984. "The Effects of Remarriage on Children: A Review of the Empirical Literature." *Family Relations* 33(3): 389–406.

Ganong, L. H., and M. Coleman. 1986. "A Comparison of Clinical and Empirical Literature on Children in Stepfamilies." *Journal of Marriage and the Family* 48(2): 309–318.

Garbarino, J. 1983. "Social Support Networks: Rx for the Helping Professions." In J. K. Whittaker, J. Garbarino, et al. (eds.), *Social Support Networks: Informal Helping in the Human Services*. New York: Aldine.

Gladow, N.W., and M. P. Ray. 1986. "The Impact of Informal Support Systems on the Well Being of Low Income Single Parents." *Family Relations* 35(1): 113–123.

Glenn, N. D., and K. B. Kramer. 1985. "The Psychological Well-Being of Adult Children of Divorce." *Journal of Marriage and the Family* 47(4): 905–912.

Glenwick, D. S., and J. D. Mowrey. 1986. "When Parent Becomes Peer: Loss of Intergenerational Boundaries in Single Parent Families." *Family Relations* 35(1): 57–62.

Glick, P. C. 1979. "Children of Divorced Parents in Demographic Perspective." *Journal of Social Issues* 35(4): 170–182.

Granovetter, M. S. 1973. "The Strength of Weak Ties." *American Journal of Sociology* 78(6): 1360–1380.

Guidubaldi, J., and H. K. Cleminshaw. 1985. "Divorce, Family Health and Child Adjustment." *Family Relations* 34(1): 35–41.

Guidubaldi, J., H. K. Cleminshaw, J. D. Perry, and C. S. McLoughlin. 1983. "The Impact of Parental Divorce on Children: Report of the Nationwide NASP Study." *School Psychology Review* 12: 300–323.

Guidubaldi, J., H. K. Cleminshaw, J. Perry, and B. Nastasi. 1984. "Impact of Family Support Systems on Children's Academic and Social Functioning After Divorce." In G. Rowe, J. DeFrain, H. Lingrin, R. MacDonald, N. Stinnet, S. Van Zandt, and R. Williams (eds.), *Family Strengths 5: Continuity and Diversity.* Pp. 190–207. Newton, MA: Education Development Center.

Guidubaldi, J., H. K. Cleminshaw, J. D. Perry, B. K. Nastasi, and J. Lightel. 1986. "The Role of Selected Family Environment Factors in Children's Post-Divorce Adjustment." *Family Relations* 35: 141–151.

Guidubaldi, J., J. D. Perry, and H. K. Cleminshaw. 1984. "The Legacy of Parental Divorce: A Nationwide Study of Family Status and Selected Mediating Variables on Children's Academic and Social Competencies." In B. B. Lahey and A. E. Kazdin (eds.), *Advances in Clinical Child Psychology.* Vol. 7. Pp. 108–151. New York: Plenum Press.

Halperin, S., and T. Smith. 1983. "Differences in Stepchildren's Perceptions of Their Stepfathers and Natural Fathers: Implications for Family Therapy." *Journal of Divorce* 7: 19–30.

Hanson, S. M. H. 1986. "Healthy Single Parent Families." *Family Relations* 35(1): 125–132.

Hawkins, J. D., and M. W. Fraser. 1983. "Social Support Networks in Delinquency Prevention and Treatment." In J. K. Whittaker, J. Garbarino, et al. (eds.), *Social Support Networks: Informal Helping in the Human Services.* New York: Aldine.

Hennenborn, W. J., and R. Cogan. 1975. "The Effect of Husband Participation on Reported Pain and the Probability of Medication During Labor and Birth." *Journal of Psychosomatic Research* 19: 215–222.

Hess, R. D., and K. A. Camara. 1979. "Postdivorce Family Relationships as Mediating Factors in the Consequences of Divorce for Children." *Journal of Social Issues* 35(4): 78–86.

Hetherington, E. M., M. Cox, and R. Cox. 1976. "Divorced Fathers." *Family Coordinator* 25: 417–428.

Hetherington, E. M., M. Cox, and R. Cox. 1978. "The Aftermath of Divorce." In J. H. Stevens, Jr., and M. Matthews (eds.), *Mother-Child, Father-Child Relations.* Washington, DC: National Association for the Education of Young Children.

Hetherington, E. M., M. Cox, and R. Cox. 1979. "Stress and Coping in Divorce: A Focus on Women." In J. Gullahorn (ed.), *Psychology and Women in Transition.* Washington, DC: B. H. Winston and Sons.

Hetherington, E. M., M. Cox, and R. Cox. 1982. "Effects of Divorce on Parents and Children." In M. E. Lamb (ed.), *Nontraditional Families: Parenting and Child Development.* Hillsdale, NJ: Lawrence Erlbaum.

Hill, R. 1949. *Families Under Stress.* New York: Harper.

Ihinger-Tallman, M., and K. Pasley. 1986. "Remarriage and Integration Within the Community." *Journal of Marriage and the Family* 48(2): 395–405.

Jacobson, D. S. 1978a. "The Impact of Marital Separation/Divorce on Children: I. Parent-Child Separation and Child Adjustment." *Journal of Divorce* 1(4): 341–360.

Jacobson, D. S. 1978b. "The Impact of Marital Separation/Divorce on Children: II. Inter-parent Hostility and Child Adjustment." *Journal of Divorce* 2(1): 3–19.

Jacobson, D. S. 1978c. "The Impact of Marital Separation/Divorce on Children: III. Parent-Child Communication and Child Adjustment, and Regression Analysis of Findings from Overall Study." *Journal of Divorce* 2(2): 175–194.

Jessop, D. J. 1982. "Topic Variation in Levels of Agreement Between Parents and Adolescents." *Public Opinion Quarterly* 46(4): 538–559.

Kelly, J. B., and J. S. Wallerstein. 1975. "The Effects of Parental Divorce. I. The Experience of the Child in Early Latency; II. The Experience of the Child in Late Latency." *American Journal of Orthopsychiatry* 45: 253–254.

Kelly, J. B., and J. S. Wallerstein. 1976. "The Effects of Parental Divorce: Experiences of the Child in Early Latency." *American Journal of Orthopsychiatry* 46: 20–32.

Kelly, J. B., and J. S. Wallerstein. 1977. "Brief Interventions with Children in Divorcing Families." *American Journal of Orthopsychiatry* 47(1): 23–29.

Kivett, Vira R. 1985. "Grandfathers and Grandchildren: Patterns of Association, Helping, and Psychological Closeness." *Family Relations* 34(4): 565–571.

Kivnick, H. Q. 1982. "Grandparenthood: An Overview of Meaning and Mental Health." *The Gerontologist* 22(1): 59–66.

Kornhaber, A., and K. L. Woodward. 1981. *Grandparents/Grandchildren: The Vital Connection*. Garden City, NY: Anchor Press/Doubleday.

Kotelchuck, M. 1976. "The Infant's Relationship to the Father: Experimental Evidence." In M. E. Lamb (ed.), *The Role of the Father in Child Development*. New York: Wiley.

Kulka, R. A., and H. Weingarten. 1979. "The Long-Term Effects of Parental Divorce in Childhood on Adult Adjustment." *Journal of Social Issues* 35(4): 50–78.

Kurdek, L. A. 1981. "An Integrative Perspective on Children's Divorce Adjustment." *American Psychologist* 36: 856–866.

Lamb, M. E. 1977. "Father-Infant and Mother-Infant Interaction in the First Year of Life." *Child Development* 48: 167–181.

Larsen, L. E. 1972a. "The Influence of Parents and Peers During Adolescence: The Situation Hypothesis Revisited." *Journal of Marriage and the Family* 34(1): 67–74.

Larsen, L. E. 1972b. "The Relative Influence of Parent-Adolescent Affect in Predicting the Salience Hierarchy Among Youth." *Pacific Sociological Review* 15: 83–102.

Lee, G. R. 1979. "Effects of Social Networks on the Family." In W. R. Burr, R. Hill, F. I. Nye, and I. L. Reiss (eds.), *Contemporary Theories About the Family*. Vol. 1. New York: The Free Press.

Leslie, L. A., and K. Grady. 1985. "Changes in Mothers' Social Networks and Social Support Following Divorce." *Journal of Marriage and the Family* 47(3): 663–673.

Leupnitz, D. 1982. *Child Custody*. Lexington, MA: Lexington Books.

Levitin, T. 1979. "Children of Divorce: An Introduction." *Journal of Social Issues* 35(4): 1–25.

Liebenberg, B. 1967. "Expectant Fathers." *American Journal of Orthopsychiatry* 37: 358–359.

Longfellow, C. 1979. "Divorce in Context: Its Impact on Children." In G. Levinger and O. C. Moles (eds.), *Divorce and Separation: Context, Causes, and Consequences*. New York: Basic Books.

Loveland-Cherry, C. J. 1986. "Personal Health Practices in Single Parent and Two Parent Families." *Family Relations* 35(1): 133–139.

Matthews, S. H., and J. Sprey. 1984. "The Impact of Divorce on Grandparenthood: An Exploratory Study." *The Gerontologist* 24(1): 41–47.

Matthews, S. H., and J. Sprey. 1985. "Adolescents' Relationships with Grandparents: An Empirical Contribution to Conceptual Clarification." *Journal of Gerontology* 40(5): 621–626.

McLanahan, S. S., N. V. Wedemeyer, and T. Adelberg. 1981. "Network Structure, Social Support, and Psychological Well-being in the Single-Parent Family." *Journal of Marriage and the Family* 43(3): 601–612.

Meissner, M., E. Humphreys, S. Meis, and W. Scheu. 1975. "No Exit for Wives: Equal Division of Labor and the Cumulation of Household Demands." *Canadian Review of Sociology and Anthropology* 12: 424–439.

Messinger, L. 1976. "Remarriage Between Divorced People with Children from Previous Marriage: A Proposal for Preparation for Remarriage." *Journal of Marriage and Family Counseling* 2(2): 193–200.

Mills, D. M. 1984. "A Model for Stepfamily Development." *Family Relations* 33(3): 365–372.

Mitchell, J. C. 1969. "The Concept and Use of Social Networks." In J. C. Mitchell (ed.), *Social Networks in Urban Situations.* Manchester, UK: Manchester University Press.

Nelson, E. A., and E. E. Maccoby. 1967. "The Relationship Between Social Development and Differential Abilities on the Scholastic Aptitude Test." *Child Development* 31(2): 234–250.

Neubauer, P. D. 1960. "The One-Parent Child and His Oedipal Development." *Psychoanalytic Study of the Child* 15: 286–309.

Nolan, J., M. Coleman, and L. Ganong. 1984. "The Presentation of Stepfamilies in Marriage and Family Textbooks." *Family Relations* 33: 559–566.

Norton, A. J., and P. C. Glick. 1986. "One Parent Families: A Social and Economic Profile." *Family Relations* 35(1): 9–17.

Norton, A. J., and J. E. Moorman. 1987. "Current Trends in Marriage and Divorce Among American Women." *Journal of Marriage and the Family* 49(1): 3–14.

Oshman, H. P., and M. Manosevitz. 1976. "Father Absence: Effects of Stepfathers upon Psychosocial Development in Males." *Developmental Psychology* 12: 479–480.

Papernow, P. 1984. "The Stepfamily Cycle: An Experiential Model of Stepfamily Development." *Family Relations* 33(3): 355–363.

Parke, R. D. 1981. *Fathers.* Cambridge, MA: Harvard University Press.

Pasley, K., and M. Ihinger-Tallman. 1985. "Portraits of Stepfamily Life in Popular Literature: 1940–1980." *Family Relations* 34(4): 527–534.

Peterson, J. L., and N. Zill. 1986. "Marital Disruption, Parent-Child Relationships, and Behavior Problems in Children." *Journal of Marriage and the Family* 48(2): 295–307.

Pink, J. T., and K. S. Wampler. 1985. "Problem Areas in Stepfamilies: Cohesion, Adaptability, and the Stepfather-Adolescent Relationship." *Family Relations* 34(3): 327–335.

Plummer, L. P., and A. Koch-Hattem. 1986. "Family Stress and Adjustment to Divorce." *Family Relations* 35(4): 523–529.

Richards, M. P. M., J. F. Dunn, and B. Antonis. 1977. "Caretaking in the First Year of

Life: The Role of Fathers, and Mothers' Social Isolation." *Child: Care, Health and Development* 3: 23–26.

Richardson, R., and C. Pfeiffenberger. 1983. "Social Support Networks for Divorced and Stepfamilies." In J. K. Whittaker, J. Garbarino, et al. (eds.), *Social Support Networks: Informal Helping in the Human Services.* New York: Aldine.

Robertson, J. F. 1977. "Grandmotherhood: A Study of Role Conceptions." *Journal of Marriage and the Family* 39(1): 165–174.

Robinson, B. E. 1984. "The Contemporary American Stepfather." *Family Relations* 33(3): 381–388.

Robinson, J. 1977. *How Americans Use Time.* New York: Praeger.

Rollins, B. C., and K. L. Cannon. 1974. "Marital Satisfaction over the Family Life Cycle: A Re-evaluation." *Journal of Marriage and the Family* 36(2): 271–282.

Rollins, B. C., and H. Feldman. 1970. "Marital Satisfaction over the Family Life Cycle." *Journal of Marriage and the Family* 32(1): 20–27.

Rosen, R. 1979. "Some Crucial Issues Concerning Children of Divorce." *Journal of Divorce* 3(1): 19–25.

Sanik, M. M., and T. Mauldin. 1986. "Single Versus Two Parent Families: A Comparison of Mothers' Time." *Family Relations* 35(1): 53–56.

Santrock, J. W., and R. A. Warshak. 1979. "Father Custody and Social Development in Boys and Girls." *Journal of Social Issues* 35(4): 112–125.

Santrock, J. W., R. Warshak, C. Lindbergh, and L. Meadows. 1982. "Children's and Parents' Observed Social Behavior in Stepfather Families." *Child Development* 53: 472–480.

Sebald, H. 1986. "Adolescents' Shifting Orientations Toward Parents and Peers: A Curvilinear Trend over Recent Decades." *Journal of Marriage and the Family* 48(1): 5–13.

Spanier, G. B., and R. A. Lewis. 1980. "Marital Quality: A Review of the Seventies." *Journal of Marriage and the Family* 42(4): 825–839.

Spanier, G. B., R. A. Lewis, and C. L. Cole. 1975. "Marital Adjustment over the Family Life Cycle: The Issue of Curvilinearity." *Journal of Marriage and the Family* 37(2): 263–275.

Spicer, J. W., and G. D. Hampe. 1975. "Kinship Interaction After Divorce." *Journal of Marriage and the Family* 37(1): 113–119.

Stack, C. B. 1974. *All Our Kin: Strategies for Survival in a Black Community.* New York: Harper and Row.

Troll, L., and V. Bengtson. 1979. "Generations in the Family." In W. R. Burr, R. Hill, F. I. Nye, and I. L. Reiss (eds.), *Contemporary Theories About the Family.* Vol. 1. New York: The Free Press.

Unger, D., and D. R. Powell. 1980. "Supporting Families Under Stress: The Role of Social Networks." *Family Relations* 29: 566–574.

Updegraf, S. C. 1968. "Changing Role of the Grandmother." *Journal of Home Economics* 60: 177–180.

U.S. Bureau of the Census. 1990. *Statistical Abstract of the United States: 1989.* Washington, DC: U.S. Department of Commerce.

Vanek, J. 1978. "Housewives as Workers." In A. H. Stromberg and S. Harkess (eds.), *Women Working.* Palo Alto, CA: Mayfield.

Visher, E. B., and J. S. Visher. 1978. "Common Problems of Stepparents and Their Spouses." *American Journal of Orthopsychiatry* 48: 252–262.

Visher, E. B., and J. S. Visher. 1979. *Stepfamilies: A Guide to Working with Stepparents and Stepchildren*. New York: Brunner/Mazel.

Walker, K., and M. E. Woods. 1976. *Time Use: A Measure of Household Production of Family Goods and Services*. Washington, DC: American Home Economics Association.

Wallerstein, J. S., and J. B. Kelly. 1974. "The Effects of Parental Divorce: The Adolescent Experience." In J. Anthony and C. Koupernik (eds.), *The Child in His Family: Children at Psychiatric Risk*. New York: John Wiley and Sons.

Wallerstein, J. S., and J. B. Kelly. 1975. "The Effects of Parental Divorce: Experiences of the Preschool Child." *Journal of the American Academy of Child Psychiatry* 14: 600–616.

Wallerstein, J. S., and J. B. Kelly. 1976. "The Effects of Parental Divorce: Experiences of the Child in Later Latency." *American Journal of Orthopsychiatry* 46: 256–269.

Wallerstein, J. S., and J. B. Kelly. 1977. "Divorce Counseling: A Community Service for Families in the Midst of Divorce." *American Journal of Orthopsychiatry* 47(1): 4–22.

Wallerstein, J. S., and J. B. Kelly. 1979. "Children and Divorce: A Review." *Social Work* 24(6): 468–475.

Wallerstein, J. S., and J. B. Kelly. 1980. *Surviving the Breakup: How Children and Parents Cope with Divorce*. New York: Basic Books.

Weingarten, H. 1980. "Remarriage and Well Being. National Survey Evidence of Social and Psychological Effects." *Journal of Family Issues* 1: 533–560.

Weiss, R. S. 1975. *Marital Separation*. New York: Basic Books.

Weiss, R. S. 1979. "Growing Up a Little Faster—Experience of Growing up in a Single-Parent Household." *Journal of Social Issues* 35(4): 97–111.

Index

achievement motivation, 74
adjustment: to divorce, 13–16, 21; to remarriage, 17–18, 87–90
adolescent-parent relationships, 21–22,
42
adult friends. *See* nonrelated adults
age-peers: age and, 23, 120–21; compared to parents, 137; divorce and,
141–42; gender and, 23, 120–21; leisure activities with, 116–17; mother's
marital status and, 127–28; support
from, 23, 116–21, 136–37
age segregation, 115
arguments, 43–45
Augmentation Hypothesis, 106–7
aunts, as supports, 103–4
authority, mothers and, 53–55
authority figures: effects of divorce on,
82–83; fathers as, 53–54, 73–74; stepfathers as, 93–94

best friends, 118–19, 121
birthdays, divorced fathers and, 85

children, as supports, 59–60
Children of Divorce Project, 14
child support, 79–80
chores, 57–59, 67–68. *See also* household responsibilities

Cleminshaw, Helen K., 12–13
competition, 131–33. *See also* jealousy
confidants: children as, 60; fathers as,
75–76, 86–87; loneliness and, 144;
mothers as, 41–43, 48–49, 78; remarriage and, 65–66, 89–90
conflict: with age-peers, 120–21; with
grandparents, 109–11; between parents, 49–50, 56–57; with parents, 43–
48, 77; with siblings, 126
contact, with divorced fathers, 15, 78–82,
84–85
cousins, as supports, 105
Cox, Martha, 12–13
Cox, Roger, 12–13

dating, 61, 119–20
decision-making, 57. *See also* negotiations
deficit model, and single-parent families,
12
Diminution Hypothesis, 105–6, 112
discipline, 53–54, 77
division of labor. *See* chores; household
responsibilities
divorce: child reactions to, 49, 51; effects
on children of, 13, 15–16; mother reactions to, 52–53; parent-child communication about, 49–50; relatives

and, 107–11; social activities and, 54, 60–61

divorced fathers, 78–87; child's age and contact with, 79, 84–85; child's gender and contact with, 80; compared to divorced mothers, 86–87; frequency of contact with, 15, 78–82; marital relationship and contact with, 80–81; mother's remarriage and, 142–43; proximity and contact with, 81; satisfaction with contact with, 82

dyadic agreement, parents and adolescents, 46–47

economic difficulties, after divorce, 54, 60–61

economic providers, fathers as, 83

family history, grandparents and, 100–101

father, absence of, 12

fathers: compared to mothers, 76–78, 137–38; divorce and support from, 138–39; social science perspectives of, 71; as supports, 38, 72–73

Fischer, Claude S., 2, 30

friends. See age-peers; nonrelated adults

Furstenberg, Frank F., Jr., 106, 112, 114

generational stake, 37, 46

generation gap, 22

geographical mobility, after divorce, 51–52

gift-giving, and divorced fathers, 83–84

grandparents: adolescent relationships with, 22–23, 98–103; as confidants, 100; divorce and, 22, 107–11, 139–40; maternal and paternal, compared, 101; support from, 98, 103

Guidubaldi, John, 12–13

Hetherington, E. Mavis, 12–13

household responsibilities, 41, 55–59, 62, 127–28. See also chores

jealousy, 64–65, 90–91, 120–21. See also competition

Kelly, Joan B., 13–15

kinship designations, and steprelatives, 92–93

kinship relations. See names of specific relations

leisure activities, 74–75, 77–78, 84–86

Lightel, Jeanine, 12–13

living arrangements, of children, 3–4

loneliness, 59, 143–44

marital dyad, primacy of, and remarriage, 64–65

marital satisfaction, 78

maternal grandparents, 101, 110–11

mediators, grandparents as, 100

mobility, after divorce, 51–52

morphology, of social support networks, 19–20, 33–35

mother-adolescent relationships: child's age and, 67; child's gender and, 67–68; divorce and, 53, 140–41; effects of remarriage on, 89–90, 142; stereotypes of, 46

mothers: compared to fathers, 76–78, 137–38; as go-betweens, 40–41; and instrumental support, 38–40, 47; as supports, 38

names, and stepfather, 92–93

NASP–Kent State University Impact of Divorce Project, 13

Nastasi, Bonnie K., 12–13

National Surveys of Children, 15

negotiations, 55–57, 67, 89

networks. See social support networks

nonconflictual relations, between mothers and adolescents, 44–45

nonrelated adults, adolescent relations with, 121–24, 129–30, 141

Nord, Christine W., 15

Northern California Community Study, 30

opposite-sex relationships, 119–20

overload, 52–59. See also role strain

parent as peer, 61

parents. *See* adolescent-parent relationships; mother-adolescent relationships; mothers; fathers
paternal grandparents, 101, 107–8
Perry, Joseph D., 12–13
Peterson, James L., 15
premature maturity, 61

remarriage: adolescent-father relationships and, 142–43; adolescent-mother
relationships and, 89–90, 142; early
adjustment to, 87–88; incidence of, 4,
16; stereotypes of, 16–17
rivalry, 90–91. *See also* competition;
jealousy
role strain, and divorced mothers, 16. *See
also* overload
rules, 56–57, 73–74, 77, 88–89

siblings, relationships with, 124–29
single-parent families: deficit model of,
12; incidence of, 3; role strain and, 16
social support networks: adequacy, 5; and
adjustments to divorce, 21; of adolescent and parent compared, 35–36; anchorage, 19, 29–30; content, 20,
31–32; defined, 1–2; density, 19–20,
31; directedness, 20, 32; and effects of
divorce, 20, 138–42; frequency, 20,
32–33; homogeneity and well-being,
144; measurement, 19–20; morphology, 19–20, 33–35; multiplexity, 20–
32, 36; size, 19, 30, 35, 138, 144; and
well-being, 144
sponsors: fathers as, 22, 106, 139; grandparents as, 107, 139
stepfathers, 87–95
stepkin, 112–14, 143

teachers, as supports, 122–23
teamwork, in divorced households, 58

uncles, as supports, 103–4

verbal skills, of adolescents, after divorce, 62–63
visitation, 78–85. *See also* divorced fathers

Wallerstein, Judith S., 13–15
weekend fathers, 83–85, 94
well-being, and network structure, 133–34

Zill, Nicholas, 15

ABOUT THE AUTHOR

KANDI M. STINSON received her B.A. in sociology from Washington University and her Ph.D. from the University of North Carolina at Chapel Hill. She has taught at Lehigh University and is currently at Xavier University, where her teaching and research interests include family relationships, gender roles, medicine and health care, and research methodology.